Praise for

The Part That Burns

"This story builds so beautifully; this voice is so confident. I love this book and am grateful it is in the world."

> —Dorothy Allison, *New York Times* bestselling author of *Bastard Out of Carolina* and *Cavedweller*

"In *The Part That Burns*, Jeannine Ouellette writes, 'Here is the thing about doorways: once you step through them you can never go back. Even if you do, you will never see the world the same way as before.' And so it is in this beautifully told, fractured memoir. Ouellette creates a house of many doorways into her broken past for the reader to step through. Each door opens into rooms painted in lush, evocative description. Our perspective shifts, our understanding deepens with each telling and, in the end, Ouellette's story changes the way we see the world."

> —Heidi Seaborn, author of *Give a Girl Chaos* and executive editor of *The Adroit Journal*

"Vital, full of energy and wisdom, Jeannine Ouellette's memoir crackles with excitement. From the shores of Lake Superior to the mountains of Wyoming to the banks of the Mississippi River, this is a story of American migration—not just of families but of spirits. I loved the brave little girl at the heart of this story, so will you."

> —Rene Denfeld, bestselling author of *The Child Finder* and *The Butterfly Girl*

"With a poet's voice and an uncanny knack for mining memory, Ouellette's memoir-in-fragments evokes pain and beauty in equal measure. Ouellette understands the elliptical nature of memory, the way years and experience can transform our understanding of the things we did as children and the things that were done to us. She loops back and forth in time to the same seminal experiences, adding layers of depth and understanding, and in so doing shows us how her wild determination to overcome the trauma of her childhood results in a life lived on her own terms. Full of love, loss, and hard-won redemption, *The Part That Burns* is a fiercely beautiful memoir."

—Alison McGhee, *New York Times* bestselling author of *The Opposite of Fate* and *Someday*

"Powerful and urgent, this is truly a book for our time: It teases beauty out of ugliness; it shows the courage of everyday survival; it creates wholeness out of fragments. With her gorgeous and precise prose, Ouellette shows that when faced with abuse we can do more than merely endure—we can fight back, we can flourish, we can thrive."

—Sue William Silverman, author of *How to Survive Death and Other Inconveniences*

"At turns tender and devastating, these essays are finely carved vignettes that, laid together, form a powerful portrait of one woman's path from hard girlhood to motherhood, the grace and mettle it takes not only to survive but to flourish."

—Melissa Febos, author of *Abandon Me* and *Girlhood*

"Jeannine Ouellette's memoir glows with incandescent storytelling centered around memories, motherhood, and resilience. *The Part That Burns* proves that life isn't lived in a linear way. Girlhood and womanhood can exist simultaneously, our former selves meeting our present selves. Ouellette's writing is ablaze with a burnished beauty."

—Michele Filgate, author and editor of *What My Mother and I Don't Talk About*

"In *The Part That Burns*, Jeannine Ouellette has gifted an entrancing and courageous story to those who have ever felt forced to silence memories of childhood sexual abuse. She is a child, searching wild, unending landscapes for doorways to other dimensions of understanding and safety. She is a young wife, then a young mother, hypnotically looping back again and again to make sense of the memories that won't let her go. Like lacy tumbleweeds finally uprooted and taking to air, this too is a story of flight. Her flight on black-as-space country roads; her flight to reach a faraway mother figure who once said she cared; and the flight of her deepest-down words, finally taking to air for those who must hear them. This is a story about giving voice to all the pieces of one's life, rendered with devastating beauty, heart, and artistry."

—Diane Zinna, author of *The All-Night Sun*

The Part That Burns

a memoir in fragments

Jeannine Ouellette

Published by Split/Lip Press
6710 S. 87th St.
Ralston, NE 68127
www.splitlippress.com

ISBN: 978-1-952897-06-1

Cover design by David Wojciechowski

Cover art by Kelly Popoff

Editing by Kristine Langley Mahler

For the ones who so bravely chose me—as long as I'm living, and longer

Table of Contents

"There is no past; there are just versions of the past."

—André Aciman

Four Dogs, Maybe Five

Mom and her sausagy little dog are hunkered down in Duluth now. When I last visited, she was giddy about a fancy new leash she'd gotten—a soft ropy thing meant for a giant breed. Mom has a cairn terrier. "Feel it," she said, holding out the leash. "Isn't it something?" She crooked her arm and laughed into her sleeve, like she does.

Mom's dog also had a dapper plaid jacket and fancy boots. Fancier than Mom's. Fancier, too, than the duplex she had rented, sight unseen. "I've contacted the authorities," Mom assured me. "The community here—they won't stand for it." She's mostly riled up about water seeping in from the eave above the tub. "And these filthy blinds," she said. "It's uncouth." Mom's crumbling front stairs are another sore spot, though she's untroubled that they rise from the shadow of I-35. "There's a little park," she said, pointing to the overpass. "With a stream. We like that, don't we?" She directed this last bit at her old dog. But the dog was snoring, soft belly splayed upward.

In the mid 1960s, not long before I was born, I-35 cost my paternal grandmother her house. "Highway robbery," Nana always said. She nursed this wound like strong whiskey until the day she died. Nana was working class, but she had expectations: a full icebox, clean drapes, a decent davenport. The right not to have her house bulldozed from under her.

Expectations can be slippery.

Mom grew up on the fringes of Duluth in a neighborhood called Smithville. She lived with her parents and four siblings and Tot—an "old maid" aunt. And, in winter, chickens. "A whole upstairs full," Mom always said when she told her stories. "Imagine the squawking. Imagine the chicken shit." This was the 1950s. Indoor plumbing was widespread, but Mom's family still had an outhouse. They also had an uncle who sawed a house in half, roof to mortar, and a cousin who filed his eyeteeth to points. Drinking was a pastime. Mom was orphaned at seventeen, the same year she got pregnant and married my father. After she divorced and remarried, Mom got the hell out. I wonder if she and my stepfather—as they shot west with us for "all the oil jobs"—laughed at Duluth's iconic '70s billboard: *Will the last one to leave Duluth please turn out the light?*

Not until decades later, at the age of sixty-eight, did Mom get headstrong about moving back "home." She set to work selling her condo in the heart of Minneapolis, where she'd long lived. Long enough, in fact, that she owned the condo outright—a sunny, hardwood sort of place in a gracious brick building. "Fire trap," Mom said. And the park across the street? "Crime pit." With her daughters in Minneapolis, along with six of her seven grandkids, Mom had no one left in Duluth. "I have a niece," she said. "And Facebook friends. I don't need any ruckus. I need peace and quiet."

I wonder, did Mom ever expect the many moves that hole-punched our childhood to end with more peace? More quiet? She never said so. Mom taught us that when small things go missing—her favorite hairbrush with its yellowed bristles, her wide black comb, her silver sewing scissors—you look for those things until you find them. "Look harder," she would say. "Use your goddamn eyes." But when big things go missing—men, houses, dogs—you don't ask questions. You don't mention it again.

You simply move on.

ONE

Pete, Mixed-Breed, Stray

I'm not in my bed or even my pajamas—I have the kind with feet now, a present from Jack Daddy. Jack Daddy is my real dad, but I don't say that to Mama. Anyway, I'm still in my favorite dress, the one with the ruffled skirt, even though it's definitely nighttime. It's black outside. It must be fall. It's not winter. In Duluth, if you open the door to winter, you know it. Lake Superior is the reason. This lake is too big, too deep. And our city is high north, almost as high as north gets. We are carved into the rocks. The cold never leaves here—not all the way.

Like I said, it's fall, not winter, and I am four years old. We are in the green house on the steepest hill, the house before we move to the gray one on Twenty-Fourth Avenue. At the gray house, we will have a corner store with a dusty wood floor and penny candy and a screen door that bangs. Mama will let me walk to the store by myself, because I will be five and then almost six. At the gray house we will get a braided rug and some macramé plant holders. Rachael will be born. She will be half of my sister. I will learn to rock her when she cries because her crib will be in my room. I will learn to wring out her dirty diapers in the toilet. "It doesn't stink when you love someone enough," Mama will say. I will try to love Rachael more.

But all of that is in the next house. On this night, in the green house on the steepest hill, a little dog barks outside our door, and Mama opens it to let him in. Mafia says it's okay. Mafia's real name is Mike, but no one calls him that. They call him Mafia because of him being Italian. If Mama is mad at Mafia, she calls him Michael, in that voice. I call him Daddy because Mama says so. But to myself, I sneak and call him Mafia like everybody else.

The little dog is whiter than sugar, whiter than teeth. He's soft.

Two black spots stretch across him—one covers the side of his face. His ears are long and black. His tail is a feathery white fan. A fancy lady could wave it in front of her face to make a breeze. But no one wants a breeze now, not even fancy people. The doggie shakes and cries.

"Poor doggie," I say.

"He's a mutt," Mama says. "A little cur." She rocks him like a baby.

Mutts are not as good as the real dogs you can buy with money. Real dogs have real names, like *collies* or *poodles* or *bulldogs*. Mama and Mafia name this mutt Pete. Mama says Pete is her dog. But Pete sleeps with me. I tuck him in with his head on my pillow, but he wiggles out from under the covers and curls up at the bottom of my bed. The heaviness of him on my feet gives me a melty feeling inside. When Pete kisses me on the lips, his tongue is warm and tickly. "Jesus *Christ*, Jeannie," Mama says. "You'll give yourself worms!"

Mama laughs her hardest when Mafia teases Pete. But when Pete bites Mafia, Mama says it's Mafia's own fault for roughhousing. The scar on Mafia's nose is silver, like the edge of a dime. When Pete barks at the front door, it is my job to open it and let him outside. Outside is where the street is. When Pete stays gone for days, I think it's because he got run over by a car. But Mama says don't worry, dogs are smart. "Smarter than people," she says. Dogs aren't always smarter than people, though, because lots of times Pete poops on the carpet. It's my job to pick up the poop. Mama calls it an accident. Then she rubs Pete's nose in it and hits him with a shoe.

This is how you teach a dog.

TWO

Brandy, Golden Labrador

Brandy is not a stray. We get her from somewhere. She is a kind of dog called a *golden lab*, so she is real, not a mutt. Brandy is bigger than Pete. Her fur is short and wiry and she smells sour. I don't know what else to say about her.

We don't live in Duluth anymore. The house on Twenty-Fourth Avenue where Rachael was born was our last house before Wyoming. Wyoming has mountains and cactuses and barbed wire but almost no lakes or trees. Our town is Douglas, and our house here is my favorite house ever. I have my own room with a cozy slanted ceiling. But then we move to Casper, where our apartment is in the basement of our landlady's house. Her name is Cecelia and she lives upstairs with lots of fancy dolls she makes out of dish-soap bottles. These dolls are the kind you only look at. No one is allowed to play with them. In our basement, the carpet is squishy and makes my socks wet. That's why I mostly play outside in the yard with something called a tetherball. I'm getting very good at tetherball. But now we are moving again to a brand-new house on Meadowlark Lane. It's square and yellow and nice. It was supposed to be even nicer, but the salesmen were crooks. Across the street is my friend Sheila, whose house matches ours, only backward. Sheila is eight, like me.

Here are things that happen on Meadowlark Lane: Mama and Mafia get purple satin sheets. Rachael turns two and has a strong will and needs to learn to behave. Jack Daddy sends me an FM radio for Christmas, and I start listening to KATI every day. KATI is the best station, and my favorite songs are "Here Come the Clowns" and "Someone Left the Cake Out in the Rain." Also, Mama and Mafia start looking for a tapestry. They talk about it in special voices like the voices people use in church. That's why

I think a tapestry must cost a lot of money. I can't believe we are getting something so nice. But days and days go by and I don't see any tapestry. I decide to ask Mama about it when she is frying onions. I'm standing behind her, getting up my nerve, when she spins around. "Christ," she says. "Don't sneak up on me like that. You'll give me a heart attack."

"I was wondering about the tapestry?" I say. "Do you know when it will come?"

"Stop using your sing-song voice," Mama says. "And stop wringing your hands. The tapestry is hanging right there on my bedroom wall." She smiles. "Go look with your eyes, Jeannie." I walk down the hall to her room, and I can't believe it, but I won't cry. It turns out a tapestry is just a dumb rug with weird pictures of people and horses.

———

Brandy and Pete run free behind our house. Back there, you have emptiness all the way to Casper Mountain—it's just greasewood and short grass, plus millions of sagebrushes. Old sagebrushes are hard and twisted but baby ones have nice soft hairs. Mama says Wyoming is ugly, but I think she's not looking with her eyes. Some cactuses have tiny flowers. If you stand still, you might see a lizard or some bright yellow birds. You might even see a jackalope. But probably not, because jackalopes aren't real. My favorite thing behind our house is the smell—dark and peppery with something sweet I don't know.

———

If something bad happens and only you see it, it could be your fault. Like when Pete slinks home whining and Mama gets down on her knees to look underneath him. Mama's nylons have a run. Sometimes she uses clear fingernail polish to fix runs, but it doesn't work for holes. "That's a big bruise he's got here," Mama says to Mafia. Her pretty round bun is falling loose, and strands of hair cover her face. I like to watch Mama in the bathroom when she twists her thick hair up, holding the bobby pins in her mouth so she can use two hands. "Look at that, will you?" Mama says now. "I think this dog got hit." On TV, the person is guessing the price of onion soup. I don't like onions, but I watch anyway. Some kids will blurt things out just because they're scared. But not me. I can keep secrets. Like how on my way home from school I saw Pete run across Albert Street, how the red car screeched, how Pete made that high, sharp sound.

———

Our house was the third one built on Meadowlark Lane. Now the workers are building taller ones that Mama calls two-stories. I guess those houses have bedrooms upstairs. The tar truck rolls out more and more street like a sticky black ribbon. Still, we don't have trees. Mama's mad about that—plus our baseboards are peeling off and our kitchen floor is bubbling up. Mostly, though, she's mad about the water in our basement when it rains, the way it flows in from those tiny windows by the ceiling, and seeps up through the floor like in our apartment at Cecelia's. Except here, the basement floor has no carpet to soak up the water. We have to soak it up ourselves with towels and mops.

Here are other things in our basement: a furnace, old furniture, boxes. Mafia's bed. That's because he works graveyard shift at the plant and sleeps during the day. It's also because he fights with Mama and raises his fist. He says he's changing, but Mama says he's not. Sometimes I sleep in the basement, too. Mama calls it being kicked out of the family. "You need to shape up," she says, "and learn to appreciate what you have. You need some respect for authority." If I don't shape up, Mama will tell my teacher what I'm really like. This scares me more than black widows or rattlesnakes or thunder or any other thing I can think of. I am my teacher's favorite—my whole class says so. I never want my teacher to know what I am really like. So, I am trying my hardest to shape up for Mama. When you're kicked out of the family, you're not supposed to sleep on Mafia's bed. But I wouldn't do that anyway. I just spread blankets on the floor by the bookshelf. I am allowed to leave the basement in the morning to go to school as long as I go straight back down when I get home. Mama and Mafia eat supper with Rachael. Rachael is too little to get kicked out of the family. She only gets spanked. In the basement, I listen as supper sounds sink down from above, strange and cottony: Mafia's voice, chair legs thumping on the carpet, dishes clattering. When the sounds stop, supper is finished. Now I can come upstairs to make my own supper. I am supposed to hurry. Mama pretends I am invisible while I boil my noodles. I like to put on tons of butter and salt. Buttered noodles are easy to make and fast to clean up. Plus, you would not believe how good they taste. Way better than real supper.

The oil plant leaves a smell on Mafia. I get the idea to pick my nose and wipe it on his jean jacket. I hate Mafia because he tried to pick me up by my hair. He can't get hold of my hair now, though. That's because Mama cut it short again. She said it was a rat's nest. Sometimes Mafia chases me and tickles me and takes off my clothes and rubs between my legs, just like he did in Duluth. I don't like this game. Not in the basement or upstairs. But upstairs is definitely better.

What happens after Easter is mostly bad. Mama and Mafia get in their biggest fight ever. He smashes the china cabinet from my Nana, and the roll-top desk, and the spindle rocking chair. He pushes Mama out the side door into the garage and throws the cedar chest out after her. The chest's metal latch slices Mama's foot open. "Help me!" she yells. "Get the neighbors!" I run back into the house and Pete runs after me through the broken furniture and out the front door. I run down our driveway, past our purple car, across the street to Sheila's house. Sheila's dad comes to the door and I start yelling—all choppy from panting—*"He-elp! My da-ad is ki-lling my mo-om!"* Sheila's two little brothers press their mooncake faces against the screen.

"Sorry," Sheila's dad says. "I don't think we should get involved in this."

Mama is outside now, stomping down the sidewalk. Her sliced foot leaves blood splotches. Mafia holds Rachael, who is squirming and whining. Mama climbs into the purple car and slams the door. The engine starts. Then, Mafia plops Rachael on the hood of the car, and now she screams for real. Sheila's dad is not looking through his screen door anymore. No one is. Mama gets out of the car and grabs Rachael. "Son of a bitch," Mama says to Mafia.

The next day, Mafia goes to work at the plant and doesn't come back. Brandy goes somewhere, too. I don't know where.

Pete stays.

I still pick up his poop.

————

Mama brings us on one of her long drives, like she does. We go all the way past the edge of the city. "Country roads," Mama says. She drives and drives and we get a little lost but Mama doesn't seem to mind. She looks pretty with her hair pulled back under a blue bandana. On the radio is "Hey, Jude." Finally, Mama parks under some low trees with branches growing straight out instead of up. Next to the trees, a small creek. "Worthless trickle," Mama says. She misses the creeks in Duluth. Rachael stomps in the trickle while Mama and I sit under the tree. Mama smokes her True Blues. "I should learn to paint," Mama says. Smoke slips out of her nose in soft white puffs. "Not everyone has a gift. But I might." She flicks her ash. "How about we girls keep driving? Like gypsies. Like thieves in the night." Mama's lazy eye is doing that thing. She had a patch when she was little, but it didn't work all the way.

"We should!" I say.

Rachael yells something, too, but I don't know what. She doesn't understand, anyway, so it probably doesn't matter.

Mama smokes another cigarette. "Well, Jeannie-Beanie, it's

getting chilly," she says, then stubs her cigarette into the hard dirt. "Let's hit the road." Rachael sticks her arms up at me—*Ketter! Ketter!* She's three now, and this is how she asks to be carried. She sits on my lap in the front seat next to Mama. "Sit still," I say. Her wet pants are soaking through my jeans. Lines of barbed wire zoom by outside the open window and Rachael's baby hair tickles my face. I do want to thieve away, partly. But, partly, I was looking forward to fifth grade. The big yellow sign for the Kawasaki shop flashes at the bottom of our hill.

We are going home to Meadowlark Lane.

Mafia comes back.

Brandy never does.

THREE

Charlie, Pekingese

Mrs. Crimshaw knocks on our door. She is holding Charlie, our Pekingese puppy. "Looks like he got in a fight," Mrs. Crimshaw says. Mama takes the dog. "Good luck," Mrs. Crimshaw says. Mama shuts the door.

"Jesus," Mama says. "This is real bad." Charlie's lower jaw is all wrong—it's dangling like a shingle.

"We should take him to the vet," Mama says.

"And pay for that how?" Mafia says.

Now we live in a big gray house near downtown Casper. Mama said it was high time we moved somewhere decent. This house is a two-story, with a real upstairs. It also has a dining room separate from the kitchen and a fancy garbage compactor. "Don't monkey with that," Mama says when I touch the garbage compactor. "You'll get your hand ripped off." There's also a porch on the front of this house and a deck in back and giant cottonwood trees and a garage filled with old clothes that other people left behind.

Jack Daddy knows we moved. I already saw the small white envelope on the dining table, the one where the shape of a check shows through. Seventy-five dollars, I think, because I have looked inside one of these envelopes before. On the same day Mrs. Crimshaw brings Charlie to our door, Jack Daddy calls from Minneapolis. He says I might go visit him at Christmas. Christmas is a long time away.

———

Charlie is spiritless. But if I pet his back and don't touch his head, he'll lick up tiny driblets of cream-of-mushroom soup. That's what Mama says to feed him. "Just a few bites," I coax. "It will make you strong." Charlie's mouth smells terrible. I try to love him more, but it's not working. Then comes the afternoon when I put Charlie's soup in his bowl and call and call for him, but he doesn't come.

"Where's Charlie?" I say to myself.

"Whe-ere's Char-lie?" Mafia says back. He spits on his handkerchief and cleans his glasses. He looks at me in that way. I am ten now. I go upstairs, where the bathroom has a lock.

———

The next things that happen are regular, like Mama going to work during the day and coming home at night and Mafia going to work at night and sleeping during the day and smoking cigarettes under Mama's Boston ferns in their macramé hangers and me looking for doorways. Doorways are formed by tree branches arching overhead. You can step under them into new worlds. You can even slip through on accident.

I get the idea for building my stairs on accident, too. I'm dragging out the trash, which is leaking because the bag tore open in the compactor. Outside, the wind is full of October, all warm bread and old leaves. I'm dragging the trash through that good air when I notice the painted blue boards sticking out from under the deck. I wonder who put them there. Or maybe they've been under the deck all along, like the old clothes in the garage. What the other people left here is mostly junk—but not these boards. These boards are perfect.

Stairs are hard to build, though. I'm making a god-awful mess with a coffee can of nails and Mafia's claw hammer. Luckily, my fifth-grade teacher says not everything has to be perfect. I lean the boards at an angle against the chain-link fence between our house and Mrs. Crimshaw's. That's when Mafia opens the sliding doors, comes out on the deck.

"Did I say you could use my hammer?" he says. I step lightly onto a clean blue board. "Get back in this house," he says. I wish I had built the next stair. "I'd suggest you listen," he says. The wind snaps my hair into my eyes. I'm growing it out now because Mama doesn't cut it anymore. I pull my cotton sweater tight around me and look over the fence to Mrs. Crimshaw's house, past the high branches of her cottonwoods, all the way to Casper Mountain. I wish I could see right through the mountain to the other side, where the long silver sky disappears.

———

One morning before school, Mafia takes me to Mama's bedroom. He pulls down my corduroys and rubs his hands between my legs like he does. He doesn't do the chasing and tickling part. Mama's dresser faces the foot of her bed. It has two white doilies on it. On one doily, a fancy brush and comb and mirror. On the other, two figurines with their arms outstretched. The bases of both figurines say, "I love you this much." Mafia finishes. I listen to his footsteps going down the carpeted stairs into the hall. Next, the closet door opening and closing. Then, the front door. I do not know, as I watch from Mama's bedroom window, that when Mafia drives away in his red truck, he will keep driving all the way to Duluth.

"Good riddance," Mama says later. Still, she cries.

Mafia and Charlie are both gone.

But we still have Pete.

FOUR

Trixie, Scottish Terrier

I don't think Trixie counts. She's Debbie's dog. Debbie is Jack Daddy's wife in Minneapolis. Their new kids are Jason and Janie. Maybe that's why Mama says it's Jack Daddy's turn. If he has new kids, why not me? She's sending me to live with him at the end of the school year. At first, I was surprised about this in a bad way. Really bad. But after I thought about it a little more, I realized it could be good, because of how Jack Daddy is rich. At least, I think he is. He owns a whole apartment building that he rents to other people, while he lives in his own separate house. He also owns two shops called Moped America and Moped World. Jack Daddy really likes mopeds.

Mama's moving to Minneapolis, too, because they have a real university there. It's supposed to be better than Casper College, where she takes her night classes now. Casper College is close to our house on Hanway Street, where we moved after Mama sold the gray house. Now she works as a naked model for the Casper College art department. I know because I find the naked drawings in her underwear drawer. Anyway, college will be easier for her without me, except she's keeping Rachael. Which doesn't make sense, because I am Rachael's main babysitter. But Mafia doesn't even call Rachael on the phone, so she probably can't go live with him.

When school gets out, we hit the road. Mama drives the purple car with Pete. Mama's boyfriend, Spider, drives the U-Haul. Spider is nice. But Spider's brother, Mike Smith, is my favorite of Mom's boyfriends. Before we moved out of the gray house, Mike Smith used to hire me to clean his trailer for ten dollars. It wasn't that hard, except for the hairs in the bathroom and his naked-lady magazines on the living room floor. The hairs, I tried not to touch with my bare hands, being careful with the rag. The magazines, I also tried not to touch with my bare hands—I pushed those under the couch with my foot. Sometimes I washed and ironed Mike Smith's shirts at our house for twenty-five cents each, minus the money Mama took for soap and water. "And electricity," she said. "It's not free, you know." I only once burned a shirt with the iron. I didn't know how to fix the mark, so I stuffed the shirt under some trash in our garbage compactor. Mike Smith never asked about it.

Like I said, Mike Smith is my favorite. Mama's other boyfriend, the one she met at Casper College, is Frank. Him, I cannot stand—he got Mama started with her belching thing. Anyway, Spider's not driving all the way to Minnesota. He'll trade off somewhere with Mom's brother Orville, who will drive until Council Bluffs, where Uncle Ed will take over. Uncle Ed is married to Mama's youngest sister, Flossie. Flossie is not rich, but when we stop at her house in Council Bluffs, she buys me a brand-new curling iron with steam. She even lets me pick out one of her old lipsticks to keep.

———

Mama and Uncle Ed drive me to Jack Daddy's in the U-Haul. His house is called a split-level. It has three bedrooms upstairs: one for Jason, one for Janie, and one for Daddy and Debbie. The middle floor has the front door, a living room with a real grand piano, and a kitchen. Downstairs is partly underground and has big windows facing the front yard, plus an office for Debbie and a giant family room with low black shelves that stretch all the way across one wall. On the shelves are Debbie's encyclopedias, which I am glad about because Mama has encyclopedias, too, and I like to read them. Also on the shelves, Debbie's special art things and lots of pictures of Jason and Janie. Across from the window is a big black couch. Next to the couch, a little cushion where Trixie sleeps. My room will be below this downstairs, in the basement—but this basement is different from the ones in my other houses. Those had tiny windows up by the ceiling where light got in, but this one is all the way under the ground, with no windows at all. "Turn the light off and you won't know if your eyes are open or closed," Daddy says. He laughs. Then he sets up my bed.

———

Mom—that's what I call her now that I'm in junior high—is moving into a weird place called student housing. "The rent is cheap," she tells me on the phone. "Just one thing, though—no dogs allowed. But you don't have to worry. I found a very nice farm for Pete." I'm sitting in Debbie's kitchen at the fake wood table. She is cooking something called Swedish sausage in her electric pan. I hate Swedish sausage. It's a slimy skin tube filled with mushy meat filling.

"Where is the farm?" I ask Mom, swallowing down something sour in my throat. But now Mom is talking about Rachael's first-grade teacher. With Pete at the farm, Rachael is all Mom's got. Except Uncle Ed. Mom says Uncle Ed's not going back to Council Bluffs after all, even though Aunt Flossie still lives there with their kids. What else to say about Uncle Ed? He has a bad back and doesn't work. His hands shake. Now he lives with Mom.

I don't know if I want to visit Mom and Uncle Ed or not. I don't know if I have a choice.

———

"Tell me something," Debbie says one Saturday morning. She is sitting at the kitchen table, pushing and pulling a spoonful of strawberry yogurt in and out of her mouth. Each time she pulls the spoon out, she sucks a little more yogurt from it. Mom never buys yogurt, or at least she didn't while I lived with her, but Debbie always does. She gets the fancy French kind with foil tops. This morning Debbie is wearing shorts and her feet are bare, so I can see the white stripe where her Dr. Scholl's sandals usually go. Yellow sun slants through the kitchen window, even though September is almost over. I'm trying to get the hang of my new junior high, which is ten times bigger than my school in Casper. All the other seventh-graders seem older than me. Every single girl feathers her hair. With my steam curling iron, I can almost make my hair feather, but it never stays. Debbie is still talking to me, still pulling the spoon in and out of her mouth. "So?" she says. "Why do you think she's doing it?"

"Who?" I say. "Doing what?"

"Your mother," Debbie says. "Living with her sister's husband?"

———

Even my friend Kim from next door notices that Debbie doesn't like me. Like how she puts notes on certain foods—yogurt and raisin bread and chocolate covered pretzels—notes that say, "Do Not Eat." Or how the day before yesterday she yelled at me, the crazy kind of yelling, for playing her piano. Not that I know how to play—I don't. But pretending is still fun. Was fun, that is. I won't be pretending on her piano again.

"It's not that Debbie doesn't like you," Kim's mom says. She's been crocheting what I think might be a shawl while Kim and I complain to her. Actually, Kim is doing the complaining for both of us, but it's me her mom looks at now, as her fingers keep working all by themselves. "It's just hard for her, you know," Kim's mom says. "She told your dad she didn't want this, didn't think it was a good idea, your coming here. It just wasn't the life she had planned for herself, or for her children. We can all understand that, can't we?" She glances down at her needles, frowns a little. "So, it's really not about you, Jeannie. At least, that's what Debbie told me."

———

Jason is smart. He's only four and can read already. He says *pass gas* instead of fart and *bowel movement* instead of poop. Janie is three and goes to baby ballet every week. She likes to visit my basement bedroom and look at my things. She especially likes when I curl her blonde hair. Debbie doesn't have a curling iron because her hair is naturally curly. Sometimes Janie and I color pictures. Mostly, though, she likes to play paper dolls. I spread out the pages on the floor and cut out the clothes. Janie chooses which outfits to put on which dolls, then I help her fold down the paper tabs. "You're good at paper dolls!" she says. But I'm not. Paper dolls are tricky. For one thing, they don't stand up because their paper stands are too flimsy. For another thing, as soon as you try to make paper dolls do anything, their bodies bend over. Sometimes their necks break. Always, their clothes fall off.

Janie sucks her pacifier most of the time. I used to suck a pacifier when I was a baby. Actually, I sucked it when I was a kid, too. Mom says she had to put vinegar on it to make me stop. Janie reminds me of myself, a little. Sometimes Daddy mixes our names up because Janie and Jeannie sound almost the same. Janie also looks like me. I saw this when I was flipping through Debbie's encyclopedias and found an old baby picture stuck in the middle of the S section. I thought the picture was Janie, but the name on the back was definitely mine, written in Mom's cursive. Also, the date said 1970, and that's way before Janie was born. It's weird if I think about it too much. Especially because of the way all this sounds like I believe Janie and I are alike. I definitely don't.

I know we're completely different.

———

Eighth grade is exactly like seventh grade, but worse. The school year is almost over by the time my health teacher, Ms. Nick, shows us that movie about good touch and bad touch. The part about bad touch catches me off guard. I have never thought about things this way, but now, after this movie, I can't stop remembering Mafia. Ms. Nick says we're supposed to tell someone about bad touch. But I'm not sure. The Mafia stuff was a long time ago, all the way back in Wyoming. And Duluth. I was little then. Does it even matter now? I'm pretty sure it doesn't, but for some reason I can't shake it out of my head. I guess that's why I finally tell Kim about the tickling game. "Eww," Kim says. "That's gross."

"I know," I say, "but do you think it counts? Like, for what Ms. Nick said after the movie?"

"Sure," Kim says. Kim is more popular than I am, so I trust her judgment on these kinds of things. On all things, actually. She is kneeling on her bed, digging in her purse for a lighter. She pulls out a yellow Bic and flicks it, holding her eyeliner in the flame until the pigment softens. Then she leans in so close to the mirror that it fogs with her breath as she rims her eyes with layer after layer of black.

I'm still glad I asked Kim about the Mafia thing. But mentioning it to Mom is a big mistake. Right away, she says something to my dad, and suddenly Debbie *really* doesn't like me. I know because of my birthday.

What happened is that my dad came home from the moped shop with a chocolate cake from Cub Foods, the kind with the clear plastic dome over it and fancy frosting with decorations. I was surprised, seeing that cake. I guess I figured we'd skip my birthday, considering Debbie's mood and everything. But my dad came home with that cake, and after supper he set it on the table with some paper plates while Debbie loaded the supper dishes into the dishwasher. Jason and Janie went up to wash their hands and brush their teeth in the upstairs bathroom, which they do after every meal. That's Debbie's rule. I had already cleared my place, so I sat back down in my spot. Dad was sitting down, too, by then. We were waiting for Debbie and the kids—or at least, I thought we were. But when Debbie turned around from the dishwasher and walked back toward the table, she just kept going, right past us and up the stairs. "But I want *cake!*" Jason was saying as the bathroom door clicked shut and the tub water started running. My dad and I held very still. So did the cake. I didn't know what to say, and I guess he didn't either. He just picked up the knife, cut two fat slices, and started eating his in great big bites. It was like we were in a play together, the two of us, pretending it was someone's birthday, pretending we were celebrating, hoping the audience believed us.

———

Luckily, Janie still likes me. She is almost five already, and I am trying to teach her to read, like Jason. She's not catching on, though. I don't know why. I feel a secret spark of joy that Janie might be stupid. Then again, I know these kids are way too lucky for that.

Anyway, it's May now, school is almost over, and my social studies country report is due. I am on my bed trying to draw a map of Spain when Janie appears at the top of my basement stairs in her pink leotard. "Hi, Janie," I say. The thing about Spain is that it has a very irregular shape, with a million little indents. It's very difficult to get it right.

When I look up from my map again, Janie is still standing at the top of my stairs, watching me. Debbie must have washed Janie's hair today, because it is so full of static that it forms a kind of blonde halo around her head. Sometimes I fix Janie's hair before ballet.

"Watcha doing?" I say.

She twists her legs around each other, raises her arms above her head in a circle. "Fifth position," she says.

"Nice," I say. "Want me to curl your hair before you go?"

"Mommy says I can't," she says.

"Can't get your hair curled?"

"Can't go in your room."

Janie chatters on, her smooth little face tilted sideways. But I can't hear what she is saying, because of the rushing in my ears. It's extremely loud, even though the air outside my body is still. Nothing moves except for Janie's round mouth, opening and closing, with her tiny teeth, so square and so white, more perfect than I will ever be.

———

I am thinking about how tomorrow is the last day of school when my dad comes down to my basement. He stuffs one hand into his pocket and pushes his glasses up his nose. His glasses are the kind that change depending on the light. Since they are still black from the sun, I guess he just got home from the shop. "I've been think-ing," he says after all the regular things he always says, like how was school and did I finish my homework and how is my friend Kim doing. He's leaning against the wall a little, shifting his weight to the left. "I think we can make things a little easier for everyone," he says.

"How?" I say, even though I already know what he will say next, about me moving out after school is over, going to live with Mom and Rachael and Uncle Ed in that apartment. He will talk about how it might be nice for me to see Rachael more. How I will be able to help Mom since she's so busy with graduate school. Things like that. Mostly I'm not listening, though. I'm watching his glasses, instead, the way his lenses are gradually losing their tint, so I can see how his eyes are looking not at me, but past me, toward the wall, as if there is a window. "It will be a good change for us all," my dad says. "Yessiree Bob, it will."

I want to fight, but I don't know for what. I don't want to live with Mom. I don't want to live here either. I picture Janie's little teeth. I don't want to live anywhere.

I never see Pete again.

And I was right about Trixie.

She definitely doesn't count.

FOUR

Smokey, Keeshond (kayz-hawnd)

Years later, I will ask Rachael, "What was that gray dog's name? The one on Brompton Street?"

"Smokey," she will say. "The cat was Bandit."

"We had a cat?"

"How can you forget these things? Smokey and the *Bandit*!"

But that's later. Now, I am fourteen, moving back in with Mom at the weird student housing place where she still lives. Rachael is eight. "Where's Uncle Ed?" I ask when my dad drops me off. Rachael shrugs. Mom's graduate school has something to do with city planning and public affairs. Apparently, it's stressful. That's why we eat so many bean burritos. Rachael hates bean burritos. I guess stress is also the reason Mom starts kicking me out of the family again. But student housing has no basement.

The first time I'm kicked out is on the Friday of the first week of ninth grade. My algebra book lies open, spine broken, on the wet grass where it landed next to my English notebook when Mom threw my stuff out the door. I pick up the book, the notebook, but now what? My legs are numb and loose, like they're not quite connected to my body. They're moving but I can't feel them. I see Keely and Lannie riding their Big Wheels down at the end of our building, by the laundry room. I've been babysitting Keely and Lannie a lot since I got here. They say I'm their best babysitter. Their mom says so, too. Her name is Eve and she is extra friendly. I think this is why I start floating off the sidewalk onto the field, moving slowly over the grass to where they live. Their apartment is straight across from ours.

Today the field is so big. When I finally stand outside Eve's screen door, she swings it open and hugs me before I can speak. That's when I cry. Later, Eve spreads a sleeping bag on the floor of the girls' bedroom. "My home is your home," she says.

The weekend is not as bad as I thought it would be. I feel weird here, but it's kind of okay. On Monday, Eve gives me lunch money, even though I am pretty sure she is probably just as broke as Mom. After school, she asks about my day. "Any cute boys?" she says. On Wednesday, I help her make egg rolls. I have never eaten egg rolls before. Every night, I write more sections of my autobiography, an assignment for English class. It's lucky I started on this assignment before Mom kicked me out, because I already copied down a bunch of things I don't remember from my old baby book, which I found in Mom's closet. She has one for Rachael in there, too. I'm also helping Keely and Lannie with their homework, which makes me think of Rachael. I have to push that thought away or I can't breathe.

It helps when Eve starts telling me how wonderful it is to have me here, how helpful I am, in a voice that sounds real. "Your mom just needs a little space, hon," she keeps saying. Eve is from Georgia, and I love the way she talks. "It's hard for your mom since Ed left," she says. "But she'll come around. Meanwhile, you're another daughter to me. Don't forget that." She kisses my forehead. Maybe it is that night, or the next, or a week later, when it happens, long after we're all asleep: red light swirling through the bedroom window, voices rumbling at the front door, two little girls holding hands beside me in their thin Disney nightgowns, crying.

Mom has called the police, reported me as a runaway, reported Eve for harboring. There is nothing to do but follow the officers to the flashing squad car and fold myself into the backseat. The officers drive me the half block to home, their police radio crackling and murmuring in the dark.

The next time I get kicked out of the family, it is spring, and Eve's family has moved away. Neighbor kids tell Rachael that Keely and Lannie left suddenly for Mexico—some city called Cuernavaca. There's a big language school or something, like maybe Eve's teaching English there, but the neighbor kids don't really know. I wonder—if I could somehow get to Mexico, find Eve there, could the police still bring me home? I'm pretty sure not. But it doesn't matter. No one knows Eve's new address or how to reach her.

So I stay with my ninth-grade Spanish teacher, instead. To have my teacher know about my real life is even worse than living it, but I have no choice. It's especially embarrassing because my teacher is also my friend Heidi's mom, so now Heidi knows, too. I wish I were invisible, like Mom used to pretend I was, but I'm not. I'm here. This apartment is nicer than ours, because my Spanish teacher lives in the newer part of the student housing complex, where the units have carpeting instead of linoleum. I think maybe my teacher is letting me stay here because I am her top student. I think her idea of me is better than the truth, even after whatever Mom tells her—which is definitely bad, because of the look on my teacher's face when she hangs up the phone. "Listen," my teacher says when I cannot stop crying. "Listen, your mother—I'm worried she has, or she might—no, let me try this again. I'm saying I wish I could do more, I wish there were better options. But as far as getting you through this—you just have to understand it won't last forever. I know that's hard to see right now, hard to believe. But please trust me, because it's true. You'll be eighteen before you know it, and the minute you are, every single thing will be easier. Easier and better. It will." She puts her hands on my cheeks, leans in. "Te prometo," she whispers. "Te prometo. You know what that means, right?"

"You promise," I say.

"I promise *you*," she says. "I promise *you*."

Heidi is in tenth grade, one year ahead of me. She clears some space for me in her bedroom, and shares everything. Even her bathrobe and all of her nail polish—dozens of bottles in every color. She calls me her new sister and teaches me to love sunflower seeds and Jolly Ranchers. Heidi still likes me, even knowing I'm kicked out. A gigantic relief. Still, some things you just know. Like how Mom will eventually call the police again, how the police will take me home again, how it will all happen exactly the same way the next time. After four times, maybe five, I open an encyclopedia to a map of North America and trace a path from Minneapolis to the Texas border. *My home is your home. You're like another daughter to me. Don't forget that.*

What happens when I do finally look for Eve gets so mixed in with other memories of that year that it seems like one long complicated dream: the time the night burglar empties our refrigerator and steals Mom's purse from the coffee table, only inches away from where I lie sleeping on the couch. And the time I oversleep and miss the bus to tenth grade once, twice, three times, and so on, until I finally stop trying to go to school, and instead walk—with money from my part-time job at Arby's—to the corner store, where I buy sour cream and onion potato chips and Twix bars and Tab, which I will bring home after Mom leaves for campus. I will bribe Rachael to stay home, too—*share my candy*, I will say—and we will play backgammon for so many hours of so many days that I begin dreaming of shaking dice, stacking chips, doubling the stakes. And the time Mom invites me out to ice cream but instead drops me off at the Bridge for Runaway Youth and drives away, laughing. And, finally, Mom's worst spell, where I convince my boyfriend, Cyrus, to drive Rachael and me to Duluth so Rachael can stay with her grandparents. "You should go," her grandparents say when they open the door to us. They look stricken. "Legal trouble," they say. Rachael's father—their son—is being prosecuted for felony sex crimes against his new stepdaughter.

Somewhere during this mash-up, Mom graduates—which is supposed to make everything better. She gets a real job, full time, at the transportation department downtown. She buys a small brown house on Brompton Street, in the prettiest little neighborhood I know, the one straight up the hill from student housing. "Yay!" Rachael says. Rachael is happy because she gets to stay at the same school with her friends. We both love this neighborhood. I spend hours wandering its winding streets the way I once wandered behind Meadowlark Lane in Wyoming. Instead of dry, open fields of sagebrush and greasewood, everything here is cheerful houses, front gardens, and boulevards shaded by oaks and elms, tall branches arching overhead.

On Brompton Street, I find *The Hundredth Monkey* on Mom's shelf and learn how scientists taught one group of monkeys on a remote island how to wash sweet potatoes, and how that new behavior spread to the island's other monkeys through observation, which the scientists expected. What they didn't expect was how, once enough monkeys—one hundred or so—learned how to wash their potatoes, the practice would jump instantly to monkeys on other islands. That's called collective consciousness, and I guess people have it, too.

I also learn about nuclear winter, and wish I hadn't. I learn that a woman can run for vice president, but she cannot possibly win, even though I spend hours and hours after school knocking on doors for Mondale and Ferraro. Other things I learn: Mom's house loan includes something very bad called a balloon payment, which I don't understand. Mom's coworkers at the transportation department are out to get her, which I don't believe. Heat and water can get turned off, which I tell to no one.

Also, Mom is spending time with one of her professors. He never comes inside, just picks Mom up and takes her somewhere for a night or two. Until he stops coming. We don't know why. But then Mom crawls into her bed and starts crying. She does not stop. The crying turns into a kind of wailing. Rachael starts sleeping in my bed with me. This must be around when Mom brings home Smokey—Bandit, too, apparently. Maybe Smokey comes before Mom gets fired from the transportation department. Maybe after. Maybe the balloon payment is looming. Maybe it's past due. What we all remember is the pizza.

"Why don't you order one," Mom calls from behind her bedroom door.

"What kind?" I ask Rachael. She's eleven now. I am seventeen.

"Pepperoni," Rachael says.

Mom comes out to pay the pizza guy. She carries the box to the dining table. She opens the cardboard cover. "What's this?" she says, in that way. Rachael's eyes dart to me.

"Pizza," I say.

"You think you're so goddamned smart," Mom says.

Rachael's hair has grown out long and smooth. She has the end of her tight braid tucked into the corner of her mouth.

"What's the matter with you?" Mom says. "Why don't you answer me?"

"What's the matter with *you*?" I say. "Why are you so crazy?"

Mom has a good arm. The pizza box hits just under the molding. Wide, shiny streak of sauce and grease down the yellow wall.

"Nobody cares that I don't *like* pepperoni pizza," Mom is saying. Her lazy eye gets going. I stand up.

"*Bitch*," Mom says.

Her hand comes toward my cheek. I lurch backward and slip around the table. I see her grab the ceramic jug from the built-in. I watch myself duck toward the kitchen. The vase smashes into the wall.

"Mom!" Rachael screams.

Mom is in the kitchen now. She has a cast-iron frying pan. "You've always been this way," she says. The frying pan crashes into the cupboard behind me. The only way out is through the dining room, but Mom is blocking. I see both of us, Mom and me. Behind us, the window, the backyard of creeping charlie, the stone wall. Beyond that, the river and downtown.

"Get out of my way," I say.

"You," Mom says. "I should have aborted you when I had the

chance." She grabs the electric mixer.

"Mom!" Rachael screams. "You're hurting her!"

"I'll kill her," Mom says.

"I'm calling 911!" Rachael is sobbing now.

The mixer hits me on the shoulder.

"Hello?" Rachael says. She hiccoughs loudly into the phone. "My mom is killing my sister." Rachael yells this right before throwing up on the dining table.

The cops, when they arrive, talk first to Rachael and me. We have been waiting outside. They are so friendly. After they go into the house, their deep voices carry through the closed window. Mom's shouts carry, too. She yells about how I am incorrigible. Launches into her latest graduate school spiel about the *community* this, the *community* that, expectations and responsibility, her usual nonsense about respect and authorities. The cops come back out, frowning. "Do you girls have family in town?" Something about "terroristic threats." They cuff Mom and walk her to the squad car. I so badly want to say the right thing to Rachael. Like, maybe, I'm sorry. But I can't. So I tell her a knock-knock joke. Years later, paging through Mom's blue spiral notebook (half notes from *Human Relations and Social Justice* and half diary), I will cry when I learn that as Mom hunches into the backseat of the squad, she wets her pants.

Mom loses the Brompton house.

Rachael and I go to foster care.

Smokey and Bandit go to the pound. I don't remember that, though. Only Rachael does.

MAYBE FIVE

Wolfie, Cairn Terrier

"They're so cheerful and busy," Mom said. We'd been seeing more of each other since I got married, had babies. And now she was going on about puppies again. She had been going on about them ever since my son Max started first grade. Sophie was nine already, and Lillie—still fuzzy-haired and babyish—was four. They would all love a dog, I was sure. But Mom focused her puppy craze on Max alone. "A boy needs a dog," she said. "A dog will give him a sense of responsibility, a sense of his place in the community. A dog will teach him something about the power of authority tempered with restraint." *Seriously?* I turned away from her, pretending to fiddle with something on the counter. But that's the thing. She *was* serious, without a trace of irony. I sucked in a breath. I rolled my eyes.

But also . . . I remembered Pete's warm body in my old twin bed. His white fan tail. The "farm." Maybe the timing was right for a dog. John and I had been married ten years already. We had recently settled into our forever home in that same quaint University neighborhood I loved, the one where Mom had bought and lost her brown house. *Cairn terriers get their name from hunting and chasing rodents between the cairns of the Scottish Highlands*, the dog book said. Feisty little dogs with outsized personalities. "Doesn't that sound perfect?" I said to John.

I got Mom involved with presenting the puppy at Christmas— after all, it had been her idea. Out on the porch, I lowered the dog into a wrapped box that Mom would carry into the house at the last minute so the kids could see the little guy pop out under the tree. He didn't pop, though. He ambled, black eyes curious and brave.

From *The Art of Raising a Puppy* by the Monks of New Skete, we learned that dogs respond to names that end in long vowel sounds, so we called him Wolfie. And we tried to follow the monks' advice on crating. We really did. But Wolfie despised his so-called safe, cozy den. "Look," I said to John after too many sleepless nights. "Our babies slept with me when the books said let them cry. The books were wrong. How much can it hurt to let Wolfie onto our bed?" *This will cause behavior problems in your dog later,* the monks promised. But in truth, things were going mostly fine. Wolfie loved the kids, loved our shaggy yard, loved that rubber Kong thing. He tolerated puppy school. I trusted he'd eventually learn not to eat paper, bark at shadows, yank the leash. Meanwhile, puppy love reigned.

But the things that happened next were mostly bad. I struck a match, and John poured the gas. That's the simplest way to tell it, and the way I generally tell it now. I used to emphasize how I didn't have an affair. Technically, I didn't. I used to emphasize that what happened was more than attraction. I fell in love. Now, I know that's worse.

Fire's first stage is known as "ignition"—and recognizing ignition presents the best chance of suppressing or escaping the fire. I wanted neither. After ignition, fire enters the growth phase, and only once all combustibles have ignited is the fire fully developed. Fully developed fires are the most dangerous for living beings trapped within.

Wolfie was distraught. When John moved out, I had to go to work full time, which meant that Wolfie—not even one year old—had to be home alone, all day, every day. Soon, he grew too anxious to sleep at night. Not in his crate, not in my bed, not anywhere. Wolfie took to peeing on Sophie's bed—with her in it. He wrecked the couch. He learned to jump onto the dining table. He learned to open cupboards. I swear he learned to sneer. Next came teeth. "It's bleeding, Mama," Max said, holding out his finger. *Some terriers are known to nip children,* confirmed the dog book. *They are also difficult to train.*

Finally, Lillie's dress. I'd found it at Marshalls and splurged with money I didn't have, for her kindergarten fall festival. Lillie, the baby. She was unraveling in our newly scorched life. But the dress—it had a red velvet bodice and a tulle skirt that landed just below her knees, both skinned. "Mama, do you love me?" Lillie said, twirling in circles, skirt billowing. "Am I a tree princess?" She arched her arms overhead. "Am I *sooooo* beautiful?"

The night before the festival, we set our things out for the next morning: kids' backpacks zipped by the door, lunches in the fridge, my tote bag on the counter, the dress draped neatly over a chair in the dining room.

You know how this ends. The monks were right about everything, even that rat's nest of tulle we found on the dining-room floor in the morning. Lillie fell to her knees when she saw it. The sound that cleaved from her was deep and low. My own sorrow, however, was too full of rage for tears. Our brokenness was more than a dress—I knew that. But a dress was all we had, and there it was, shredded by that little cur.

That night, I called Rachael. She was grown and out of foster care by then, forging a family of her own. At first, she'd been scared about my divorce—*You're going to lose that house! You're going to end up like Mom!*—but she'd settled some now.

"Get rid of that dog," she said.

"I can't," I said. "You know that."

"Mom could take it."

"Mom? With a *dog?*"

"You're gonna come apart, Jeannie. And you can't do that. You just can't. Your kids need you."

"Seriously, though? Mom?"

"She can do this one thing," Rachael said. "She has her disability income. She's home all day, with zero responsibilities. She can step up." Before disability, Mom had worked odd jobs—telemarketing, mostly—but not anymore. She had nothing if not spare time. Still, I couldn't ask her. I wouldn't ask her. But my sister did. "Listen," Rachael said to our mom. "You have to help with that dog. You have to."

Fire's last and longest phase is decay. I waited years to marry the man I'd fallen in lust then love with—still, smoke lingered. Still, it lingers. The phoenix is just a cliché. But some organisms really do survive by fire. For example, fire lilies are coaxed open only by smoke—nothing else will trigger their blossoming.

Mom never did give Wolfie back to us, no matter how often I asked. "Not now," she'd say, laughing into her sleeve. "He just started a new diet." Or, "Another dog moved into the building—a new friend for him." Or, "He's too stressed with this heat. Let's wait for fall." Wolfie's walks and mealtimes, his girth, his maladies—real and imagined—and, of course, his shenanigans, became the warp and weft of Mom's days. So, we did what we could to help from a distance. We hauled Wolfie to vet visits, nodding dutifully to lectures about overfeeding. We gave Mom rides to places she wanted to go with Wolfie, when she couldn't take him on the bus. And we brought Wolfie to our house when Mom had something else going on—though, admittedly, that was rare. Except, that is, for the Fourth of July.

Until Mom moved back to Duluth, we always had Wolfie with us for the Fourth, otherwise he would fall apart over the fireworks in the park across from Mom's condo. Mom would start calling me mid-June to firm up a plan, to make sure I wouldn't forget about my commitment to Wolfie, my promise to protect him from that kind of suffering. "You don't know," she would say, "how much that poor dog hurts with any kind of commotion. He's sensitive, Jeannie. And gentle. The slightest clap of thunder, and you would cry yourself to see how he shakes and shivers." Mom says Wolfie became so distraught once from some construction noise in the building that he didn't eat for two days. "He just can't stand such ruckus," Mom always said. "I'm telling you, he cannot. This little dog, he needs his peace and quiet."

Tumbleweeds

Western Jackalope (*Lepus Tempermentalus*)

I don't believe in jackalopes. But people have to make up their own minds about these things. Douglas, Wyoming, is the jackalope capital of the world. A jackalope is a cross between a male jackrabbit and a female antelope. Jackrabbits and antelopes are both real. With real things, you don't believe or not believe. They just are.

Douglas is the jackalope capital because it's where the first jackalope was spotted by a trapper named Roy Ball in 1829. So maybe jackalopes existed back then. But it's 1975 now, and supposedly jackalopes are extinct. Still, people report sightings in Douglas all the time.

I love our house in Douglas. It is white and green with a cozy front porch that juts into our little square yard of brown grass with one spicy pine tree. Inside, wooden stairs lead up to my bedroom, which has a slanted ceiling and peeling wallpaper that smells of fire and old books. Next to my bed is a square-paned window, glued shut with paint. Pine boughs scratch against the glass when the wind blows. In Wyoming, the wind always blows.

In the middle of downtown Douglas, in front of the old train depot, is a giant statue of the jackalope, painted gray and white. The statue jackalope looks friendly, like the Easter Bunny. But jackalopes are not friendly. They're fighters. They use their antlers to attack and gore their enemies, which is why they are also called warrior rabbits.

I learn these things in Douglas. I also learn that we are foreigners. Foreigners have accents, which means I sound funny when I say things like *house* and *rag* and *I want to come with.* I learn that most kids in my second-grade class don't believe in Santa, and that some schools, like Douglas Elementary, have no walls. I learn that if Mama cuts your hair very short because your face is narrow and you don't look nice with long hair like other girls, your teacher might not know who you are. She might say, "And who is our new boy in class today?" I learn I have a talent for dirty looks, and that sometimes Mama thinks my looks are funny and sometimes she says, "Get that look off your face before I slap it off." I learn there are some things I can't change. For example, the look on my face. But other things, I can change. Like the way I talk. It's not that hard.

Jackalopes can change their voices too. They can even imitate human voices. Mafia loves jackalopes. He says he sees them on his long drives to and from the graveyard shift at the oil plant. The word *graveyard* makes me imagine a cemetery, like the one at the top of the hill in Duluth where Mama's parents are buried in the ground. But, really, Mafia's job is something about uranium. It stains his hands. Whenever we drive past the plant at night, I press my forehead against the cool glass of the car window and watch for the shadowy shapes of the oil buildings with their millions of twinkling lights.

"In the days when cowboys sang by the campfire at night, the jackalopes sang back," Mafia explains one dusty afternoon. He blows smoke out of his nose. "Jackalopes like to sing before thunderstorms, too, because they can only mate when lightning flashes. Their milk is a love potion."

"Is that right?" Mama says. She and Mafia are at the kitchen table, drinking their coffee. She holds my baby sister, Rachael, on her lap.

"You bet it's right," Mafia said. "The jackalope is sometimes called the horny rabbit."

Mama laughs into her sleeve. "Little pitchers," she says. Rachael is the one on Mama's lap, but Mama is talking about me.

"Little pitchers should empty this ashtray." Mafia picks up the gold dish from the kitchen table and holds it out. "Go on, Jeannie-Beannie," Mama says. "Don't be a beast." I carry the ashtray through the kitchen to the back porch, where the garbage can is. I spill some of the fluffy gray ash onto the floor, accidentally on purpose.

Mafia doesn't like me, except for the tickling game. It goes like this: Mafia chases me, I run. He catches me, I yell and shriek. He tickles me—under my arms and behind my knees, under my chin and between my ribs. I shriek more. He pulls my clothes off and puts me on his lap and rubs his hands between my legs. When he stops, the game is over. That's how it works. I was four when I first learned to play. Once you learn, you don't forget.

One way that jackalopes escape hunters is by imitating a human voice. A jackalope might call out trick phrases—*There he goes!* and *Quick! Over there!*—to throw you off the trail. Mafia says the best way to catch a jackalope is to lure it with whiskey. "Jackalopes love whiskey," he says. "Drunk animals are slower and easier to hunt." Mafia hardly ever drinks. Neither does Mama—not since the explosion. But I can still get away. I just pull myself through a doorway inside of me.

Some people say it wasn't Roy Ball who spotted the first jackalope in 1829. They say it was a taxidermist in Douglas who made the first jackalope in 1934. The taxidermist tossed a dead rabbit down on the floor of his shop next to a pair of antlers, then rushed off to eat supper. When the taxidermist came back, he looked at the rabbit and the antlers and decided to mount them together, just as they were. He made a fortune selling jackalope trophies. Now, the Douglas Chamber of Commerce issues thousands of official jackalope hunting licenses every year. But the hunting of jackalopes is allowed only between midnight and 2:00 AM on June 31.

Tumbleweeds (*Lechenaultia divaricata*)

A tumbleweed is a plant known as a diaspore. Once mature, it dries and detaches from its root and tumbles away.

We move to Casper because people in Douglas don't like for-eigners. But kids here say I talk funny, too. Anyway, Mama and Mafia want to grow grass in our dirt yard on Meadowlark Lane. But there are two things they don't know. First, how hard it will be for me to pull tumbleweeds out of the ground. That's because tum-bleweeds tumble only after they detach from their roots. Then the dry spiny balls—full and round and light—fly away on the wind, spreading seeds as they go. But when a tumbleweed first starts growing, it clings hard to its spot. Its tiny green leaves and dark purple stems web out in all directions. Its roots dig into the earth with a strong central core. Tendrils branch out and weave another web just under the soil's surface. At this stage, tumbleweeds hold their ground.

The second thing Mama and Mafia don't know is that some things just don't grow in Wyoming. For example, things that are tender, and thirsty—like baby grass. Tumbleweeds, on the other hand, love Wyoming. They can roll free in the wide spaces and con-stant winds. I hate tumbleweeds. They come out of nowhere and bite you. You can never let down your guard. But you might also want to be a tumbleweed. Just look at them, lacy and weightless, rising and falling on rivers of air.

Eventually, the yard is clear enough to spread grass seed. Water-ing is my job. I watch every day for tiny green hairs to poke out of the brown mud. One here, one there. Someday, I think, as I spray the hose, these hairs will spread and make a soft carpet. But day af-ter day, they do not. Eventually, I am sent to sleep in the basement as punishment for killing the grass. Mafia sleeps in the basement during the day because of working graveyard. My favorite thing to do in the basement is read his books, like Phyllis Diller's *House Keeping Hints*. Phyllis has a friendly face and says things like, "Nev-er serve meals on time. The starving eat anything."

Mama and Mafia order sod. It arrives on a flatbed truck, giant spirals of green and brown Hostess Ho-Hos. They roll it out like a carpet. I like to take my dolls camping on this new pasture. I lay them down to sleep under a dishtowel tent. Mostly, though, I wander in the dusty nothingness behind our house. I think maybe I can walk all the way to the foothills, but I am afraid I won't get back before Mama comes home from work. I ride my bike to see if I can get closer, but no matter how fast or how far I go, the distance between the mountain and me never changes. Nothing does. Dust is dry. Cactuses are sharp. Wind blows. Tumbleweeds tumble.

One day I find a hidden canyon full of wildflowers. This is the kind of place where I might find a doorway. Not my favorite kind of doorway, where two branches meet to form an arch that you can step through into another dimension. I won't find that, because there are no trees in the canyon. But maybe I could find another kind of doorway, like a circle of wildflowers where the sun casts its rays at precisely the right slant to open the door to a new world. I make my way down to the bottom of the canyon and discover a trickle of water. All around me, the canyon walls are bursting with tiny blossoms and the sweet, oily scent of sage.

But no doorway.

I come back to the canyon early the next morning with a picnic in my bike basket. I will search all day and night. I spread out my dishtowel and arrange an apple, a tuna sandwich, a thermos of orange juice, which I open thirstily. Then, out of nowhere, bees and bees and bees swarm up out of the canyon like a cloud.

Tumbleweeds can do terrible things when they join forces with other tumbleweeds. They can even swallow buildings and cars. In South Dakota, tens of tons of large tumbleweeds buried so many houses so deeply they had to be dug out by rescuers.

Western Meadowlark (*Sturnella neglecta*)

Here's what they say about the Western Meadowlark's song: it is complex, garbled, and abrupt. Its secondary call is short and buzzy, like a cackle. The Western Meadowlark is the state bird of Wyoming.

I scout for this yellow shock of a bird while wandering behind our house looking for doorways. Meadowlarks are easier to hear than to see, unless you spot one singing on a fence post. There are no fence posts back here—not like the miles of barbed wire dividing plots closer to town. I never see Indian Paintbrushes either. That's our state flower—my teacher says it is in the broomrape family. So, I know for a fact it is real.

I love the smell of raw cedar standing against the hard wind. We have a six-foot cedar fence around our backyard. Inside the fence, our sod has shriveled to patches of brown with wide-open seams, like a quilt coming apart. The fence separates us from the swath between our back door and Casper Mountain. Everyone on Meadowlark Lane has a cedar fence to hold back the emptiness.

At least five states besides Wyoming have the meadowlark as their bird, including Kansas, where schoolchildren voted for it in 1925. I believe in children voting. I love school. Mrs. Lavelle is my favorite teacher, but she is in Duluth, where I went to first grade, before we moved to Wyoming for the oil jobs. My four schools in Wyoming are Douglas, Hall, Park, and Southridge, a new one for every year. Mama and Mafia like to move.

My fourth-grade teacher at Hall keeps a kiln in her storage closet. If you get 100 percent in spelling or math, you get a ceramic animal to glaze and fire. I love my animal families. First, the biggest turtle, then the second biggest, then the baby turtles, each smaller than the next, the tiniest one smaller than my thumbnail. Then, my ladybug family, my duck family, my bluebird family, and so on. I am very good in spelling and math.

Meadowlarks make their nests on the ground. They weave dried grasses into bowls, where they lay five eggs at a time. The eggs are white, with brown and lavender spots. After two weeks, they hatch. The mother birds look after the nests and broods, but sometimes the fathers help with feeding. In six weeks, the baby birds are grown.

At Park Elementary, my fifth-grade teacher is Ms. Routson.

She lives at the Women's Club downtown. We girls sometimes visit her there on Saturdays. Before she got glasses, Mrs. Routson didn't know what things looked like. "See that?" Ms. Routson points beyond our classroom window to the cottonwoods shimmying in the dry gust. "All those little leaves shaking on the branches? I never knew that's how trees looked. I used to see only big blobs of green." Every afternoon, Ms. Routson reads to us: *Ivanhoe*, *Robinson Caruso*, *Little House on the Prairie*. One day, instead of opening the book, she passes out sheets of paper with purple ink from the ditto machine. The paper is warm in my hands and smells wonderful, like gasoline, or alcohol. Mrs. Routson says that today we will take turns reading out loud. Tracy sits in the far corner of the front row, so she goes first. "Diary of an Unborn Child," Tracy reads. "Today, my life begins."

At Southridge, my sixth-grade teacher is Harper Lee, named after the famous author. The boys say Ms. Lee doesn't wear a bra, or maybe she wears one with circles cut out of the cups so that her nipples show. I don't know how to picture this. My best friend at Southridge is Holly.

Holly gets her name from being born on Christmas Eve. She has four brothers and sisters and lives in a big house high up in the hills where we walk together after school while Mama is still at work. Holly has her own big bedroom and an actual waterbed. I get to sleep in the waterbed with Holly every time I spend the night at her house. Only a few times does Holly ask about my house, whether we can play there. "Wouldn't that be fun?" she says. "Yeah!" I say. "I'll ask my mom!" But I never do.

Holly's mother loves Princess Diana and is excited to watch the royal wedding on TV with us. Holly's father has an important job, but I don't know what it is. When he gets home from work, Holly pulls on his arm and begs him to watch our baton show in the backyard. "Please, please, please!" Holly says. We practice our batons every single day. When Holly's father watches our show, he says it is outstanding and we should take it to Broadway.

On weekends I go to church with Holly's family in a plain building that looks nothing like a church. We swallow big chunks of soft white bread and grape juice for communion. Mormons don't drink alcohol. Holly's mother drives a station wagon with wood side panels. One Saturday in spring, Holly and I walk all the way to Casper Mountain. We get so hot and thirsty we are almost scared. Then, finally, on our way up the base of the mountain, we find a real waterfall and stand under it, letting it gush over our heads and into our mouths. This, too, could be a doorway.

When a meadowlark spots an enemy, it will typically hunker down and freeze while casting a wary eye. When crouched, the bird's yellow chest is hidden. It blends into the surrounding brown. In my sixth-grade class, the girls divide into groups. I'm in the best group, with Holly and Rebecca and Karen and Nicole. Wendy used to be in our group, until we dropped her. We might let her back in, but only if Rebecca says so. Rebecca never gets dropped. I haven't been dropped yet, but only because I'm the newest girl in sixth grade. When the girls in our group say we have to drop Holly, I go along. If I don't, they might drop me instead. After we drop her, Holly looks bent over. Every day, she sits by herself, walks by herself, eats by herself.

One afternoon I see Holly's mom on the playground outside the school office. I am wearing a pair of Mama's pantyhose that I snuck from her underwear drawer. Now they sag and balloon around my knees. When I see Holly's mom, I freeze and cast a wary eye. I wonder if she might slap me. But she just opens her pretty lipsticked mouth and sounds exactly like herself when she says, "Oh, how Holly misses you! We all do. You must come over again soon!"

Brown-headed cowbirds sometimes lay their eggs in the nests of other birds, including the Western Meadowlark. Some species of birds will remove the foreign eggs, abandon the nest, or just build a new nest on top of the invaded one. But some species will raise the baby cowbirds as if they are their own.

I don't know which of these the Western Meadowlark will typically do.

Jimmy Carter *(Homo sapiens)*

James Earl "Jimmy" Carter, Jr. is the President of the United States. I am going to star as Jimmy Carter in a play written and directed by my new friend, Nora. I met Nora when we moved from Meadowlark Hills to the gray house downtown. That was right before Mafia left—like a thief in the night, Mama says. He raised his fist to her for the last time, she says.

Nora's house has a chandelier and a spiral staircase to the third floor. Her dad is a lawyer. Nora's house also has something called a sewing room, where her mom keeps bolts of fabric and boxes of thread and needles and bobbins and basting tape and cotton stuffing and so many other interesting things. A whole room for sewing. Nora even has an actual trampoline in her yard, and something called a widow's walk up on her roof, where we sit in the sun and write plays to act out later. Or at least, we used to. Now Nora is changing. For one thing, she hardly ever wants to do our plays anymore. She mostly says, "This is stupid. If you want to do a play you can do one by yourself." I always want to play at Nora's, but sometimes Nora comes here to play when Mama's not home. "We can do anything we want at your house," she says.

Jimmy Carter used to be a peanut farmer. He got elected president while I was still searching for doorways. People don't like Jimmy Carter. They say he talks funny—like us, except his accent is Southern.

I turned ten before we moved to this house, but Nora is almost twelve already. That's why she understands TV news and all that stuff about inflation and the Middle East. Nora says Jimmy Carter could solve the energy crisis with my oily hair. I start washing my hair every day. Now she says if we're going to do a play, we should do one about Jimmy Carter.

"You should slick your hair back," she says. "And talk with a Southern accent."

"Why do I have to be Jimmy Carter?"

"Because you look like Jimmy Carter. You have short hair and a manly face."

Not many people watch our plays. Mostly just Mama and her new boyfriend, Spider, and Spider's brother, Mike Smith. That's how Mama says his name—Mike Smith. Probably because my stepdad's name is also Mike, even though I would never mix them up because of Mafia being called Mafia. And because of his thieving and leaving.

We need to make everything professional and realistic.

"Your hair's not slick enough," Nora says. I hold up the cardboard box I've sawed into the shape of a TV screen with a dull steak knife and balance it in front of my face. I start into my speech about peanuts and how much I love them, how salty and delicious they are. How we could use peanut oil to fuel the nation.

Mama says the economy is going to shit. Something called a recession. Plus, Mafia being gone. We have to sell our car. The boom is over. Everything booms and busts. Mama works during the day and goes to Casper College at night. She keeps slapping me and grounding me for that look on my face. I don't like being grounded, but it's better than being kicked out of the family. The basement of this house is wet and crumbly. I do not want to sleep down there. I have been grounded most of this school year. That's why Nora mostly comes over when Mama's not home. It's not only because I don't want her to see our broken screen door or the dog poop in our yard that I forget to pick up, or because of Mama's yelling, but also because I am not allowed to have friends over, anyway. When you're grounded, you can't go anywhere or see anyone unless Mama says so. It depends on her mood.

I am old enough now to babysit Rachael, who will go to kindergarten next year. Sometimes I take her to Woolworths while

Mama is at night class. I wonder if Rachael misses Mafia, because he is her father. I have mostly forgotten my father.

Jimmy Carter gives speeches on TV. He says he has been given a great responsibility to stay close to me, to be worthy of me, and to exemplify what I am. He says we should create a new spirit of unity and trust. He says my strength can compensate for his weakness, and my wisdom can help to minimize his mistakes.

"Your hair still isn't right," Nora says. "You need some gel."

The only person in our house who has hair gel or other fancy make-up is Karen, our upstairs boarder. Karen doesn't really live in our house, though. She just stores things in our back bedroom so her parents won't find out she lives with her boyfriend, which is a sin. Rachael and I snoop through Karen's dresser and closet. Sometimes I borrow her socks, even though they are too big for me. Some of Karen's sweaters are almost my size. Rachael thinks I should borrow her bras, too, but I think that is going too far. Besides, I don't even need one. Our other boarder is Derek, and he rents the add-on room next to the dining room downstairs. Derek isn't around much, either, but his room is boring to snoop in except for his bacon-flavored crackers. Those are better than we expect.

When Derek leaves, Diane moves into his room with her little boy, Joshua. They actually spend time in our house, something I didn't realize boarders might do. One night while Mama is at night class, Diane cooks in our kitchen. Rachael and I whisper about how she puts tomatoes on her grilled cheese sandwiches. Diane and Joshua even sit at the table and eat vanilla ice cream that Diane bought. They eat it right in front of us.

Jimmy Carter says we can be better and stronger than before. He says our dream endures, and that we need to learn together and laugh together and work together and pray together.

Diane's long prayers are weird. She thinks lots of things are sinful, which we find out after Rachael tells Joshua to "shut up, you spoiled brat" and Diane makes a big stink about it. Diane tells Mama that God doesn't approve of divorced women with boyfriends and Mama tells Diane to leave and not let the door hit her in the ass on her way out. Then Karen makes a little stink about how someone is digging through her things. Rachael and I hunch together on the living room stairs as Mama yells that no one has ever once set foot in Karen's room. After that, I know we can't get into Karen's hair gel anymore. "I saw Vaseline in your upstairs bathroom," Nora says. "Try that."

Jimmy Carter says the whole world is filled with a new spirit. He says people are craving and demanding their place in the sun. We do our play during one of Mama's good moods, on a night Spider is over with Mike Smith. The Vaseline is a great touch. But the best part is my peanut speech. My accent is perfect. You can definitely tell I am Jimmy Carter. The whole audience loves it. Nora hardly has a part since she is the newscaster. I am the star. But Nora was the one who knew grownups would like a play about Jimmy Carter. So we are even.

The next morning, I bend over the sink to wash my hair before school. When I finish washing it, my hair feels just as slick as it did before I started. I have no choice but to drip through the hallway into Karen's room for her Head and Shoulders. I have used that shampoo before at Holly's house. I know it feels gritty. I hope it might sand off the grease. But it doesn't. "Maybe Comet cleanser will work," Nora says when she sees me at school.

Jimmy Carter says he has no new dream to set forth for us. That we need fresh faith in the old dream.

That night, I use Karen's entire bottle of Head and Shoulders. I hope Karen won't tell Mama, even though I know she will. Some things you just know. Like Karen will move out of the back bedroom and out of the gray house, Nora will keep changing, and I will start changing. We will move back to Minnesota. Eventually, I will do my last play. Maybe I already did.

Mother *(Mater)*

In fairytales, many children are motherless. But that's not always how it was. Snow White was originally tormented by her mother, not a stepmother. Hansel and Gretel were abandoned in the forest by their two natural parents. And one early version of *Sleeping Beauty* has the prince's own mother trying to eat her grandchildren and her daughter-in-law. It was the Grimm brothers who changed these bad mothers into wicked stepmothers.

When I grow up, I will be a mother. This is a doorway. I will have two babies—a girl and a boy—or maybe three, lined up from biggest to smallest. I will take them into the forest and toast cheese on sticks over an open fire, just like in *Heidi*. I will give them salty milk from country goats that eat straight out of our hands. In late autumn, we will decorate an evergreen with dried oranges and pinecones dipped in peanut butter and make a circle around the tree and sing to the animals to bless the long winter ahead. I will bake homemade bread from wheat I grind myself, cutting thick slices while it is still steaming hot, and I will slather the bread with creamy butter and raw honey, all the way to the crust. Then one day, in the deepest part of winter, my firstborn daughter will pull her baby brother's hair and push him headlong into the edge of the banister, and before I know what I am doing, I will slap my daughter across her velvet cheek. For a long time, I will believe this is a curse.

In fairytales, the most vulnerable women are the old ones. These crones are past the usefulness of childbearing and housework. Often, they are the family storytellers. They interpret folklore in the light of their own history and best interests. They try to sweeten up their young listeners and remind them that, however ugly and foolish and useless a crone may appear, she could also be a fairy in disguise. She could be magic.

My mother is old now. *Tell me about Wyoming,* I think of saying. *Tell me about Mafia, your purple satin sheets, how long you knew. Tell me about when you were young, before me, before your parents died when you were still a child. Tell me again about your great aunt Tot, how you pretended to fall into the outhouse over and over and how she always came running, no matter how many times you played the same trick. Tell me about the chickens that lived upstairs, and the time your uncles got drunk and sawed a house in half, and how you went off to play in the dangerous part of the woods and punctured your leg with a railroad spike. Tell me once more how you loved watching the blood spurt up in a perfect, pulsing arc.*

Here is the thing about doorways: once you step through them, you can't go back. Even if you do, you will never see the world the same way as before. Cottonwood leaves will forever shimmy singularly in the wind. It might be hard.

Someday I will return to the Wyoming of my childhood. I will roam the open fields all the way to the foothills. Forget mountains—they're too far out. In the fields, I will smell the peppery dirt. I will rub sage into my palms, my hair, my mouth. I will rip a tumbleweed from the ground and feed it to the wind.

I will visit the town of Douglas on June 31 between midnight and 2:00 AM. I will walk in the moonlight and cast a watchful eye. I will trace my fingers along the length of barbed wire that separates one plot from another. I will feel in the dark for that particular point, sharp and exact, where I turned.

Lucky Nine

"Was it good?" John asked. It was February, two months before my twenty-first birthday. Outside, the air was bright and taut with snow yet to fall. John and I burrowed under a blanket, even though the old iron radiator poured soft heat into the bedroom. So much heat we could smell the newly varnished floors. This wasn't my old cinderblock apartment near the U of M campus, the first one I rented after foster care. This was a smaller but prettier apartment that John and I rented together, now that we were together. Almost a whole year now. The apartment was on the third floor of a stately brownstone south of downtown. We could see the buildings of Minneapolis from our stoop. The neighborhood was rough, but I loved the shiny maple floors, refurbished tile bathroom, miniature galley kitchen. I loved the wavy old glass in the paned windows, the way it mottled the world.

"Snow," I said to John, pointing to the window. Sharp flakes fell not in flurries, but one at a time, straight down.

"Hey, was it good for you?" John said again. I sighed and pressed my head into his smooth, wide chest. He had never asked this question. I didn't know how to answer him. I kissed his shoulder. "Hey," he said again. He wiggled his hand between his chest and my chin, lifted my face toward his. "Was it *good*? Did you *come*?" I wanted to press my face back into his chest, but he kept hold of my chin. "One orgasm?" he said. "Or more?" I set my gaze just beyond his eyes, toward his temples, which quivered slightly with his pulse. "Two?" he said. "*Three*?" He smiled now, sat up. "Four times, Jeannie?" I let out a little laugh, one I hoped might sound like, *Oh, you big joker you, aren't you silly, haha*. But then John said, "Wait, five? *Six*?" We were too far out now—and it had happened so fast, I couldn't possibly swim back. John's brown eyes trained giddily on mine, his naked body warm under the quilt, our legs still entwined. Snow fell faster than before, long straight lines to the unseen ground. "*Seven* times, Jeannie?" John lifted my chin again. "Eight?" I tried to move my head, but I was too slow. "*Nine*?" I grabbed one of John's hands in both of mine and pressed his palm to my mouth. I growled a little from my chest, a kind of *grrr, grrr*, like a small dog, I hoped, just play growling in a friendly way. John whistled through his teeth and shook his head, slowly. Back and forth, back and forth. "Nine times," he said softly. "Nine times."

Baby Girl

His name was definitely Frank. Hers, I can't say. But the roses—those, I will never forget. Waxy, fluorescent hybrids so extreme they tipped over from the burden of their outsized heads. Some might have called them garish, but not me. I was dumbstruck by their loveliness—suspicious, even. I wanted to touch them, eat their petals, prove their reality. So thick were the roses that they nearly obscured the chain-link fence they lined, which inexplicably cordoned off a small patch of the already small backyard, itself squared in by yet another chain-link fence. In the center of the rose-lined inner fence was a concrete slab with two folding lawn chairs, the old aluminum kind with webbed seats and plastic arms. Presumably, this is where Frank and his wife relaxed on summer nights—maybe with sweat blooming in the folds of their necks, maybe with pain shining like spurs in their knees and hips—to admire their rose progeny.

"Prune them once a year and they'll go great guns all summer, every summer," Frank's wife said.

"That's right!" Frank slapped his palms against his thighs. "Prune 'em back and watch 'em go. There's nothing to it! Nothing at all."

Frank and his wife were like their roses, listed over and tilting into the tail end of this life thing, while John and I had barely arrived at the threshold. Old and thick now, these two were selling off the house where they'd raised up five kids—plus all those roses—and moving to somewhere more manageable, perhaps a first-floor apartment with walk-in closets, no stairs, and full-service lawn maintenance. Inside, the house smelled of cabbage. Outside, it smelled of toasted oats—specifically, it smelled of the Cheerios manufactured twenty-four hours a day at the General Mills factory around the corner, where Jackson Street dead-ended against Broadway, the busiest urban drag in this semi-industrial section of Northeast Minneapolis.

John and I moved into the house in August, dragging our few dozen boxes, our bed, and our one large piece of living-room furniture, a gray couch I'd gotten from Salvation Army and re-covered myself with remnant fabric I sewed by hand. Our wedding would be performed in an evening ceremony on September 29. John was Catholic, but neither of us knew that our wedding day marked the Feast of St. Michael, also known as Michaelmas. Michael was an archangel, who, according to the Book of Revelations, slew the dragon of evil.

———

The house was a two-story clapboard farmhouse with pretty leaded windows and an open porch. A slatted wooden swing hung from the porch ceiling by two thick metal chains. On those first summer evenings in our new house, John and I would sit shoulder to shoulder on that old swing, body heat and summer heat forgetting their boundaries. We ignored the traffic whizzing by on Broadway, marveling instead at the burst of lush maple in our front yard. Although shabby, our new house had the best bones of any on the block. It was very good stock for Northeast, a working-class neighborhood settled mostly by Eastern European immigrants and known for having both a church and a bar on every corner. Northeast streets are named for U.S. Presidents in the order in which they held office. "Andrew Jackson was the seventh president of the United States," John told me. "Dirt poor and orphaned during the Revolutionary War, a kid with no education from a backwater cabin in the Carolinas, and he makes it to the Oval Office. How do you like them apples?" John was twenty-five now, and a social studies teacher. He knew things. He also knew this neighborhood, having grown up a few blocks away on Madison Street. The middle school where he taught was nearby as well. John liked things to stay the same.

I was twenty-one and had grown up in two states, several cities, and more than a dozen houses and apartments, plus the two foster homes after Mom's last breakdown. I wanted to believe in things staying the same. To prepare for the wedding, I had dropped out of the college classes I had been attending on Pell grants and had taken a full-time job selling ads in the smoky, classified department of our city newsweekly. Working felt safer, and being broke had put John in a bad temper that seemed to improve in direct proportion to my paychecks. Besides, the wedding required a dress and flowers and a reception with food and alcohol and, apparently, linens, which were supposed to match what salespeople referred to as the "bride's colors." Working definitely made sense. I hated ad sales, though, despite having a knack for it. I hoped, one day, to be a writer instead. But my advertising job paid more than John's teaching salary—and here we now were, homebuyers.

Once settled on Jackson Street, I often stood alone in our cabbagy little kitchen staring out the back door into the layers of chain link. I would look through the fences and past them, like old glass, to the distortions beyond: my childhood in Duluth, that tough, cold city on the cliffs above Lake Superior, where I was born when my mother was twenty. Two years later, Mom divorced. I remember nighttime by the front door, the painted yellow banister, my dad's legs and brown shoes, a hard-sided suitcase, a pat on the head. Then Mom's new husband as I turn four. Thick fingers, secret tickling. The apartment above the Eighth Street Market, where I lick the aluminum screen door on a snowy day, tongue frozen to metal, mouth sharp with blood. Broken furniture, fists, hair. More tickling, more fists, squealing tires. Mom says never again. Again. Another divorce. Then a loud crack, something deep, an axle maybe, or a bone, or a lung, my iron lung.

———

The first big surprise on Jackson Street arrived sometime in November along with my sinus cold. I took an antihistamine to dry the infection up, but I was also practicing, or at least trying to practice, a natural birth control method that relied on me being aware of my so-called fertile mucous. Natural birth control was my idea, not John's, despite that he was a lifelong Catholic and I was not religious. What I had said, then, was that I just didn't like the pill—it made me bloated and quick to cry. Both of these things were true, and the crying aspect also combined badly with John's temper when the two collided. But there was something else, too, that I could not name. A prickling under my skin, like a phantom limb waking up. To track your fertile mucous, you have to feel things, and I wanted to feel things. Of course, I had no idea about the whole-body effects of antihistamines, how they dry you out everywhere, not just your nose. In any case, we discovered the baby would come in August, and until then, would live, astonishingly, inside of me.

I devoured every possible good thing: broccoli and whole-wheat spaghetti, horse-pill vitamins, voluminous tomes on natural birth and breastfeeding. I foreswore coffee, diet soda, sugar. But anything, it turned out, could hurt the baby, directly or indirectly, like that thing they say about chaos theory, how the oblivious flapping of a monarch butterfly on a summer afternoon can manifest weeks later as a hurricane on a distant shore. Luckily, a promotion at the newsweekly got me out of the smoky office and into my own, where the air was clean—but, still, I was an outlier in a sea of salesmen whose passions were booze and cigars. This spiked my stress, which I feared would hurt the baby, which further spiked my stress, and so on. While I tromped back and forth from work, and most of the rest of the time, too, I obsessed. It wasn't just the bad things I might do, warned the experts—it was also the bad things I'd already done. Those ignorant wing flaps I couldn't take back were already building velocity offshore. Meanwhile, more immediate threats lurked everywhere: car exhaust, mold, tuna. Plastic, pesticides, tight seatbelts. Doctors, for their potential mistakes. Water, in a glass or the tub. Loud noises. Ignorant relatives.

Cabbage. Cheerios. Fear.

———

One chilly November evening not long after the pregnancy test came back positive, we got the second surprise. Christopher, a friendly kid from down the street, showed up at our door. "She's living under your porch," he said, holding a scrawny black kitten up to the screen. He pulled the kitten close to his cheek and made kissing sounds. I opened the door. "See how scared she is?" Christopher said, thrusting his prize at me. "Isn't she little?" She was, indeed, very little. Her spectacularly tiny bones vibrated in my hands.

"What is that smell?" I said.

"That's her farts. From eating garbage."

We took the little cat in, and I named her Baby Girl, because of the way I cradled her in my arms day and night. I was practicing. I practiced at Thanksgiving too, cooking a giant turkey for John's big family. We were celebrating the holiday, yes, but also being married in a new house with a baby coming. It was mostly good until the kitchen sink backed up before dinner, which was then served late, sending John's father into a stormy mood made worse by the cranberry walnut stuffing we had concocted with thick hard slices of whole wheat bread instead of breadcrumbs from a bag.

"Whatever *this* is, it is not stuffing," John's father said.

The next things that happened were just as expected. The sugar maple in the front yard dropped the last of its leaves, the grass turned brown, and the wind turned hateful. "Better prune those roses," John said. John was always quick to do whatever needed doing. It was one of the things I loved most about him. I had never seen anything like it before, the way John got things done. With Mom, things that broke stayed broken. Grass that grew stayed long. And there were never any roses to worry about. In any case, John took care of business, and it comforted me more than he could know. Now, he hauled a hacksaw up from the basement and marched out to the concrete slab where he knelt down and, one by one, sawed off the tops of the rose bushes.

I watched from the back steps with Baby Girl purring in the crook of my arm. "Are you sure that's how you do it?" I said.

"Yep," he said. "You just hack them to the ground and they come back bigger and better in the spring. Remember what Frank told us? There's nothing to it. Nothing at all."

Through December and January and February, I toted Baby Girl around the house and worried. I made kissing noises in her ear, the way Christopher had done. I buried my face in her fur, now glossy and smooth, and whispered *I love you* and *I'm so scared*. Soon I had a high shelf of belly for Baby Girl to sling her small body across, but I couldn't feel the real baby inside me. "That's normal," the obstetrician said, "because it's your first." Meanwhile, my breasts swelled up like distant planets and my normally narrow face became moon-shaped so that when I looked in the mirror I didn't recognize myself. I found a crib and a dresser and a square blue rug at a discount store. Instead of a wallpaper border, I wanted a shallow shelf just under the ceiling, where I could line up old-fashioned toys and dainty knick-knacks for the baby to look at. As soon as I described this to John, he got out some tools and hung the shelf, just like that. Meanwhile, we attended childbirth classes where the teacher said to practice breathing in a certain way, by counting each breath going in and out while imagining my cervix opening up like a rose blooming, petal by petal by petal.

March brought the thaw, and something else too. It happened all at once one evening, as I was driving home from work, and at first I was unsure, but then it came again: a flutter under my belly button, which made me laugh and then cry out loud because of the glory that rose up and filled the car, spilling out through the wheel wells and the heater vents and the tiny fissures between the windows and their casement. There is a reason this moment was once called the quickening. Soon afterwards, as the last dirty mounds of snow ran down the gutters under the harsh March sun, I began watching for the roses to come back. Having never had roses or, for that matter, any kind of garden, I wasn't sure what to expect. When should the bushes green up? April brought my twenty-second birthday. May came in chilly. I hoped that was why the rose canes looked just as lopped off as they had after their November shearing. By June, the sun was soft and warm, the grass thick and green. The world slid gently into summer. The roses, however, remained as they were: dry brown sticks. Clearly, they had died.

What I felt was guilt.

Poor Frank! Poor Frank's wife!

In July, I sat heavy and hot on the cement stairs. Baby Girl rolled in the dust at my feet as John stomped into the backyard with a shovel to dig out the rose remains. Pruning, it turns out, is a specific art we should have considered more carefully. Shirtless and sweaty, John finished his anti-pruning, after which there lay a great pile of rose carcasses on the grass amid clumps of disturbed soil. A row of evenly spaced black holes gaped beneath the chain link, which no longer showcased the heart of the yard, but instead encircled nothing. John hurried past me toward the basement stairs. He re-emerged, whistling and swinging a sledgehammer. First he went after the fence, then the slab.

Demolition is like that. It sucks you in. It swallows.

———

There were many things I didn't know that year on Jackson Street: how to prune roses, the legend of St. Michael, and how John didn't know everything, either. (For example, Andrew Jackson made his fortune as a slave trader and then amassed more wealth on the backs of Native Americans. He bore the nicknames "Indian Killer" and "Sharp Knife.") What I did know, though, was that symbols are real, people pay for what they do, and dead roses can't mean anything good. *Please,* I prayed. *Let the baby be okay. I'll do anything. Please, please, please.*

I prayed, despite not being religious enough to have set foot in a church since the wedding. Our ceremony had been held in

John's boyhood parish with Father Earl, a flamboyant priest who'd presided there since John's Catholic school days. My mom had been brought up Catholic, as well, but was ex-communicated for divorce, for which she held a grudge. After a brief stint in the Lutheran church, which had donuts, we had tumbled out of the fold. As a result, I never knew when to cross myself or genuflect or sit or kneel or stand. I knew neither prayers nor hymns by heart.

The whole of my marriage to John was a little like church: my ignorance juxtaposed against things he already knew. Take sex. I lacked experience and didn't enjoy it, although I pretended I did, since this seemed the reasonable thing to do. John, in contrast, had been with many lovers and liked sex fine, as long as I wasn't bleeding. His efficient approach to the matter was by far preferable to the only lovers I'd known before: Milo, Bob, and Cyrus. Cyrus was first, but he was also last. So it makes more sense to start with Milo.

———

Milo was thirty-one and drove a city bus. His route included the foster home where I lived during my senior year of high school, right up until I was seventeen years, three hundred and sixty-four days old. Then, I walked out of that house, my clothes in a garbage bag, and no fear of the police. But while I was still in the foster home, I rode Milo's bus. Milo was sad for two reasons: his multiple sclerosis and his divorce. He missed his wife and his little son and daughter whom he saw only on weekends. Milo lived in a second-floor apartment where he cleaned the bathroom with the "two-square method," meaning you wipe the sink and counters with two squares of toilet paper. For sex, Milo preferred the couch to the bed. He also preferred for me to lie sideways with my back to him. Generally, I only saw Milo when my real boyfriend, Cyrus, insisted on being with other girls. After my eighteenth birthday, I never rode Milo's bus again.

———

My manager Bob was twenty-nine. I met him the summer before I started college, when Cyrus and I were in one of our break-ups.

I was raising money door to door for affordable health care and clean water. Bob had a blunt mustache and liked to sleep with as many team members as possible. He chain-smoked both joints and cigarettes. He gave me exactly one gift, a threadbare stuffed camel from his childhood, shaped like a lopsided pumpkin. When the canvassing job ended in the fall, I never saw Bob again. It took me years to give his camel to the Goodwill.

———

Cyrus was eighteen and studying to be a police officer. I was seventeen and still living in the foster home, trying to finish high school. Cyrus was half Ojibwa and wore his long black hair parted in the middle, with a red or blue bandana around his forehead, tied at the back of his head, plus black jeans and a leather vest and motorcycle boots. He drove a vintage hearse, which old people found unsettling. Cyrus played Dungeons and Dragons, for which he painted many tiny figurines. My biggest worry at seventeen, trying to be Cyrus's girlfriend, was that he already had a girlfriend named Kumi. "I will always love Kumi best," Cyrus told me. Kumi had lived in the United States as a Japanese exchange student, but now she was home in Japan. "Which means I can be with you until she comes back," Cyrus said. "She agreed to that." Maybe Kumi had also agreed to the part about Cyrus sleeping with other girls while loving Kumi best and dating me, but I felt unsure.

Cyrus lived with his mother, Alex, who was equal parts kind and exhausted. Every evening, she sat on the couch watching standup comedy and drinking white wine. "Once," she told me from her spot on the couch, "I was sitting right here eating a tuna sandwich and I nodded off abruptly. When I woke up, the cat was licking tuna out my open mouth."

By the third year of this arrangement with Cyrus and his mother and Kumi and the other girls, I had been accepted to the University of Minnesota. I could hardly wait. I would take Latin, linguistics, and poetry, women's studies, sociology, logic. I lived in a cinderblock apartment near campus and worked at an ice cream place that also served burgers and fries and beer cheese soup, which I craved constantly and with increasing fervor. It was February when my breasts finally caught fire. I had not had my period for too long a time. "I'll drive you to the clinic," Cyrus offered. On the exam table, I stared at the ceiling and tried not to see my stepfather's face. I clenched my fists and curled my toes, watching from a distance. Cyrus held my hand as we walked to the hearse afterward. And he watched carefully from the curb in front of my apartment building, waiting until my key turned in the lock of the front door. Then he drove away, honking twice. Climbing the stairs hurt, but not enough. All night, I listened to the wind, until the dark gave way to gray and then to the white-blue of morning, at which point I was exactly the same as before, except different.

Drifting away from Cyrus took time—mainly because he tried so hard to stop me. He must have seen a kind of change in me, something electric that I could not hide. Cyrus tried to change himself, then, too. He cut his hair short and bought new pants and shiny dress shoes, all things that would have otherwise pleased me. It didn't work, though. By then, I had met John while working at the university fundraising center. John was finished with his college degree and looking for a teaching job. He was also engaged to someone else, but decided to call it off and take back the ring. "Someday," John said, "I might give this to you."

————

When we started dating in earnest, John and I would take long drives to see his parents, who had moved from Madison Street in Northeast Minneapolis to a big lake house in the country. His mother was cool toward me at first, due to John canceling his wedding and such, but I loved her anyway. In fact, I loved most everything about her, starting with the way she moved about the kitchen and, at lunch time, placed checked cloths on the long table in the screen porch. There, she served the food she had prepared for everyone, including John's older brothers and sisters and all of their little children, the littlest of whom were especially fond of me.

Bit by bit, I told John things, mostly working backward from Cyrus and the clinic to Milo and Bob, to the foster homes, to my mother, to Mafia. John shared secrets, too, like how once on Good Friday he ate way too many fish sandwiches and had constipation so severe that his mother had to drag him to the doctor. And how his father had a temper, so that sometimes when he got going, one of John's four older siblings would set off the fire alarm in the house and then they would all tear around screaming, *Bob alert! Bob alert!* And how his older siblings had started him on drinking gin in the basement when he was twelve. And how his fiancé, too, had missed her period, which was especially problematic because of how they were both Catholic. And how afterward, they had promised to stop having sex altogether until their wedding, which now would never happen.

John kept a little sailboat at his parents' house. On days with wind, John would skipper us into the choppy waters of Deer Lake. He taught me the difference between the boom, the rudder, and the mast, between the bow and stern, starboard and port, fore and aft. He taught me how to work the ropes for the mainsail and lean out over the spray. Most of all, he taught me how to come about under the boom when the wind changed its mind, or he did. Sometimes John's friends joined us at the lake. On those days, we'd go out on his parents' pontoon, which, unlike the sailboat, required no effort, no attention. On the pontoon, we'd drift aimlessly, alternating between floating and swimming in the cold inner chambers of the lake and sunning ourselves on the boat's flat deck while enjoying plastic cups of spiked fruit punch. Sometimes I'd run my finger down John's calf to remind him. The shadows would stretch eastward and our faces would tighten, red and tingly from too much sun. Late in the day, we'd bring the boat back to the dock and climb rubber-legged onto the lawn. John would build a nice little bonfire in the stone pit near the shore and cook his specialty dish—an open-flame honey-bourbon chicken, blackened and sweet, which we'd all devour with more punch.

It was on one of those first spiked summer nights that I got enough alcohol in my blood to do it. I had just finished rinsing my mouth and brushing my teeth after throwing up another belly full of blackened meat. I was still new to drinking, and the world spun gently as John and I lay side by side in the dark of his mother's basement guestroom—sinfully crammed into one twin bed rather than the two she expected from unmarried couples. I reached under the cool cotton sheet and traced the curve of John's ribs. I closed my eyes, sucked in a breath. "I love you," I finally whispered.

"Thank you," John whispered back.

The window behind our bed was open to the lake, and a cacophony of cricket song rose and fell. From the utility room, the rattle of the furnace kicked in. My own breath joined that ensemble of sound as it caught and roughened in my throat.

"Hey, now, don't be sad," John said. "My saying thank you doesn't necessarily mean I don't love you. I'm just making a point."

"What kind of point?"

"That saying 'I love you' isn't like fishing," he said. "You don't say it just to hear it back. That's manipulative. Okay?"

————————

What I feared most during that year on Jackson Street was that my brokenness was—like my pregnant body—slowly swelling, and that it would spill out of its hiding place and expose me for who I really was. As a child, I had learned that although broken things can often be hidden, most will eventually be found, and few will ever be fixed. Maybe I had faked my way into a job and a wedding and a Baby Girl who was actually just a gassy stray cat, but motherhood was different. I had thought—for one hovering moment in that slant of late September sun at the altar of John's boyhood parish—that I had resolved my past, with its closed fists and thick fingers. But at twenty-one, I had not nearly grasped the wreck, the thing itself and not the myth, as Adrienne Rich so poignantly describes. I wish someone could have told me about the real surprise: how my daughter's gray, wondering eyes, when she first looked up at me that August, would become like the beam of a lamp along Rich's "something more permanent," how her sweaty little head might point me toward "the thing I had always been coming for." That would have been a comfort on those terror-stricken mornings I spent alone, staring through empty chain link.

But I had to find it out for myself, when she finally arrived, my featherless bird. The girl who breathed first under water, who lived first inside the wreck of me. She was the thing itself, more real than I could have known or dreamed. Her newborn hand—curled into a shell—was pressed to her mouth, itself a splendor, with her upper lip rippling perfectly over her gums with their delicate Epstein pearls. Beneath this yearning pink, shocking evidence of bone: a tiny chin, sharp and distinct. "Exactly like yours," John said, "but smaller." His own chin trembled then, and his brown eyes spilled the same saltwater through which we both now swam, swam madly toward this baby, whose naked body pressed tight to my chest even as the tide of her drew us farther and farther out, away from the shore we had stood upon only moments before, but now would never see again. This fathomless child was everything I had always known without knowing, everything I had ever grasped for in the dark; she was another world, humming and transparent, embracing and rocking us in her cradle of brine.

We named our baby girl Sophia, for the sheer beauty of it, and because it means wisdom. She would give her lifelong love to the first Baby Girl, wrangling that little cat into ruffled doll dresses and walking her on a leash and reading her stories and coaxing her to drink from teacups and eventually, seventeen years later, watching her die.

Maybe healing, when it happens, is the result of a quantum entanglement, the swirling of a thousand winds. Maybe it comes when you give your daughter your own heart like another plush toy she will drag with her everywhere, clenching it in her baby fists whenever she screams in fear or sadness or pain, soaring through the air with it as she jumps from a swing at the highest possible point in the July sky, stuffing it into her backpack as she skulks off to high school on a bad day, locking herself away with it, broken, when her first love leaves her. All along, I would give Sophie the best thing I had, other than my love, which was my words. I gave her all of them, filling her up as she nestled into the curve of my life. I would be awed when she grew up to be a writer, too. Decades into the future, she would read my writing, and, with utmost care, examine each word, test its shape and weight, before skipping it back across the water, counting how many times it bounced before slipping under.

―――――

Here is something else I wish I had known during that year on Jackson Street, about symbols and how we pay: symbols mean only what we say they do, and if we do pay at all, maybe it is as Baldwin says, with the lives we lead as our only currency. Here's the truth about brokenness: you can tear a thing apart and tape it back together, and it will still be torn and whole. There is no other way. Scars don't lose their feeling. They become more tender to the touch.

As for roses, it turns out there are many kinds, including old-fashioned shrubs that produce modest, five-petaled blossoms. These roses barely resemble their showier, cultivated cousins. But wild strains are resilient and hardy. They thrive through the harshest climates, enduring neglect and even abuse with surprising tenacity. They are harmed neither by lack of care nor their own adaptations. They require no pruning, yet bloom abundantly summer into fall, year after year. These roses are something like strays. You can love them, but they know how to grow themselves.

Holy Mary Mother of God

The black bodysuit was a surprise gift from John for our first anniversary, which we would spend downtown Minneapolis at the Hotel Luxe. Our first night away from our newborn daughter. I was distraught at the thought of leaving Sophie overnight with John's parents. It felt like emptying the contents of my ribcage. But the books said that to protect our marriage from distance and divorce, we needed to be a couple, not just parents. The books said we needed to try. Maybe that's why John had splurged on the body suit, ordering it from one of those lingerie catalogues. All Lycra and spaghetti straps. *Ultra-seductive*, the label said. *Enticingly crotchless.* John wanted me to wear the bodysuit while we had sex, what with the no-crotch situation. "It'll be more exciting," he said. He also wanted me to model the bodysuit for him as soon as I pulled it out of the package.

But I said no. I was too embarrassed. "I'd rather surprise you at the hotel," I suggested. I regretted that offer now, though, hiding in the tiny bathroom of our dim hotel room. I'd lost most of the baby weight, but the last few pounds kept my breasts too pendulous and my belly too soft. Even without the extra fluff, I felt too *open* from Sophie's birth. Too semi-solid, a soupy mess of genitals and organs, engorged breasts and raw nipples spraying sugary milk—actual *milk*!—across the room; milk for this baby, *my* baby, born perfect and untouched, landing in my arms, skin to skin, hide to hide against my heart, thumping, thumping. I studied myself in the full-length mirror. Turned sideways. Being black, the bodysuit did make me look slender. And I knew John would like it. But it was also just . . . weird. I opened the bathroom door.

"Hot mama!" John said. "Holy Mary, mother of God." He was

already naked except for his underwear, propping himself on the pillows against the upholstered headboard. I laughed and perched lightly beside him. Ran my hand over the comforter, hoping to be suggestive. "Get under here," John said, lifting the blankets. "Six weeks is a long time. I'm gonna come like a freight train." He pulled the black spaghetti strap off my shoulder.

"Careful, okay?" I said, then ran my hand down his inner thigh so he wouldn't think I didn't want to do it.

"Still sore?" he said.

"A little."

The episiotomy had been painful—not a straight midline cut through the thin, fast-healing skin of the perineum, but a mediolateral cut, rarely performed in the United States anymore, involving a forty-five-degree incision stretching from the bottom of the vaginal opening all the way through the thick, strong muscle of the vaginal wall. For the first week afterwards, I could not walk unassisted. I had not wanted an episiotomy at all, no matter the type. But the anonymous on-call male doctor had insisted. "Look for yourself," the doctor had said to John as I pushed through another contraction. "See? If I don't cut her, she will tear, and that will be worse, I guarantee it." I watched as John's face turned gray. "Scalpel, please," the doctor said.

Now, six weeks later, walking on level ground was mostly fine, but stairs still hurt, as did squatting to pick up Sophie's pacifier, or coughing, or sneezing, or laughing. Sometimes, I wasn't even sure what brought on the searing, that little line of fire along the incision. It came and it went.

"I'll be careful," John said as he pulled me onto the bed, wriggled out of his underwear. It's good to be loved. John kissed me on my cheek and on my mouth. He seemed so happy. So happy. He felt around for the hole in the black bodysuit. He stretched it open and guided himself inside me. He thrust deep. Tears rolled into my ears and hair. The walls fell away in four directions.

"Still okay?" John said.

I clenched my teeth. I curled my toes.

The Part That Burns

The woman next to me is moaning—a low, wet gurgle from under her ribs. I shouldn't hate her for this. But I do. "I could whip out a gun right now," the moaner says during her turn to speak. She looks at me, points her finger. "I could shoot you." She moves her finger-gun slowly around the circle, pointing at each of us. "I could shoot you all. Bang, bang, bang."

I look away. I don't believe this woman has a gun. I don't believe she will shoot me, or anyone. Still, I root myself into my chair, resist the urge to smooth the denim of my maternity dress where it has wrinkled on my lap, where I've been gripping it in my damp hands, twisting. It is a cold March, and I am five months pregnant with my second child. Third, if you count—but here's the thing: I was eighteen at the time, fresh out of foster care, and the father was a car thief. Also, a gunrunner. Not that I knew about the cars or the guns until years later, when I Googled him and saw his mugshot. He was in federal prison by then. Anyway, I'm pregnant with my second child.

She's breathing loudly through her mouth, this woman beside me. I try not to spin my wedding ring around. I've been married to John for almost three years. Our daughter, Sophie, will be two in August. I was twenty-one when John and I married. He was twenty-five and already had his teaching degree by then—also his own car. Check, check. Stable family, too—his parents were still married—and not wealthy but, you know, middle class, I guess. No criminal record. Check, check, and check again. John also had a fiancée whose name was the same as mine, except spelled differently: Janine instead of Jeannine. Uncheck, I guess, and question mark? Things mean things, but it's hard to know exactly what. My wedding ring is a yellow gold band, the kind that overlaps in front, so that the small diamond—the same diamond John took back from the first Janine when I said I couldn't see him if he was engaged—more or less floats between the two ends of the band, which don't actually meet to form a circle but, instead, go off in their own directions. Modern. John had gotten my ring custom-made downtown at the same place where he had purchased the original ring. The jeweler melted the gold from the first Janine's band, made it into mine, and reset the diamond. I stare at the ring now to stop myself from moving my hands, or any other part of my body. Speaking of my body, it is heavy in this folding chair, even though I myself am not heavy. I myself am weightless, like fire, floating up near the ceiling, which is brown with water stains.

A body is made up of parts—bones, fascia, tendons, muscles, nerves, viscera, skin. Parts are made up of cells. My cells are vibrating. I hold my breath to stop the vibrations. The baby inside me kicks, and I slam back down into the folding chair. In the corner of this dim room, a space heater rattles. Our group leader is speaking now to the moaning woman with her gun finger. Our leader is saying, over and over, "Shh, it's okay. We're all going to be okay." But the moaner just keeps moaning, making more of those gurgling sounds, wetter than before. I try not to look, but I do. Tears stream down her cheeks and drip onto her red T-shirt, spreading into inky dark splotches.

Now the older woman across from me is speaking, because it is rightfully her turn. She says, "My father—it was almost every night those years. And my sister. I couldn't keep him off her. I'd have taken him twice, I would have, if"—now she blows a stream of air through her thin lips. "My sister killed herself last year." Another woman, the thin one with hands so chapped they bleed, says nothing at her turn. She just stares down into whatever she sees in the frayed fibers of the gray commercial carpet.

We meet in the basement of Trinity Lutheran, our support group for adult survivors of incest and childhood sexual abuse. On the cusp of twenty-four, I am the youngest in the room by far. My therapist told me I should attend these meetings. As for her, well. I found her in the Center City yellow pages under *counseling* when I couldn't stop the thoughts of Mafia. Not since that night I was pulling Sophie—like I said, almost two already, and suddenly so much easier to see as the child she will soon be at three, at four—pulling her from the sudsy water of our old claw-foot tub, grasping her tightly under her arms, all silky slipperiness—and realizing how perfect she is, and therefore how perfect I must have been at her age, too. As I held Sophie's squirmy body, that was when Mafia started coming at me again—the way he did back in the rocky city of Duluth, in the green house on the hill above Lake Superior, and after that, Wyoming, where we moved for Mafia's Exxon job, first to Douglas, then to Casper, and, when it all fell apart, back to Minnesota again. But Wyoming—it's the Mafia of Wyoming I remember most vividly, Mafia of the high wind and sharp tumbleweeds, the mountain and the shadow of the mountain where he left his mark. Mafia came back that night as I held Sophie close to me, and now he's hunkered down to stay, all settled into my body with his basement bed and oily jean jacket. I can't stand it.

So here I sit on a metal folding chair in the lower level of Trinity Lutheran, hating this woman with her tear-splotched T-shirt, her threats and her moans, her stupid finger-gun. Hating her for being exactly like me—ruined—but letting it show.

———

Sophie's hands are starfish. They open and close and grasp for me. Her eyes are full of ocean. The world swims inside her. When she sleeps, her face turns into something else, something far away and otherworldly. Only a year ago, her top lip still had a white blister from nursing, which she did greedily and with her whole body until her head would loll back, and bluish-white milk would dribble down her sharp chin and pool, sweet and sticky, in the shadowy spaces where her skin met mine.

Now Sophie is finished with nursing. It feels too soon. But

here we are. She drinks cow milk and watered-down apple juice. She eats baby cereal with sliced bananas, soggy noodles with butter and salt, Cheerios and rice cakes. She even eats raspberries from the bushes in our yard. How she loves raspberries! She loads them into her mouth by the fistful. But in spite of all this nutrition, Sophie's hunger for me has not ebbed. She is voracious for me, in fact. Ravenous for my attention in any form, but especially in the form of stories. For her, I have become a story hunter. I find stories mostly outside, weaving together bits and scraps we find on our long walks through the neighborhood.

We take these walks often because—well, here's the truth: Sophie can be a cantankerous and demanding child. *Spirited,* is what the books say. *Spoiled,* is what John's parents say, wrongly. Sophie is smart, is what she is. Smart like a sponge. She soaks everything up until she's too full, then she spills over. When that happens—when she becomes overwrought, thrashing on my lap, refusing comfort, tearing off her clothes, pillaging her room and ransacking her toy chest like a burglar, and it is all too much for her to bear—I chase her down and stuff her back into her clothes and then her jacket and hat and finally into our hand-me-down stroller so I can push her along the heaved-up sidewalks of this sleepy little town we share with five hundred neighbors. We moved here to Center City, forty-five minutes north of Minneapolis, during Sophie's first winter. Most days I cannot believe we live in this beguiling place. I push the stroller along the crest of Summit Avenue, past the other Victorians. Some, like ours, are sturdy but in need of love. A few are going to ruin. Several, though, are simply glorious with their gingerbread trim and their wide, welcoming porches. I love our street, our town, our house.

At the end of Summit Avenue is the historic stone church with its magnificent steeple, and beyond the church, the isthmus between North Center Lake and South Center Lake, a strip of land so narrow you can see the open water behind the houses on both sides of the street. I push Sophie past the county jail—a discreet cinderblock building that strikes me as being not much bigger than our living room—then past the rows of tiny, colorful bungalows that line this tucked-away road. So removed is this enclave, so hidden from the rest of town, that it feels like trespassing just to be here. For Sophie's sake, I invent stories about the people in the bungalows—the man who sews tiny shirts from milkweed and soft strips of birch bark in the hope he might someday have an infant son to wear them; the woman who stays up late into the night when the moon is full because she hears the singing of her long-lost sister in the waves breaking against the shore; and the little girl, "just like you, Sophie," whose flying doe is strong enough to carry her all the way across North Center Lake while also shrinking small enough to slip inside a mitten. Sophie listens hard to my stories. Her big brown eyes spin and her jaw muscles contract rhythmically, as if she is chewing my words and swallowing them down.

———

"Hey," my therapist says to me in the middle of Brink's Grocery. I am pushing a cart with Sophie in the child's seat swinging her sturdy little legs as vigorously as possible in order to make her snow boots fly off. I have already stuffed those boots back onto her feet four times. Today is one of those April afternoons in Minnesota when the world goes green around the edges even while the ground is still covered with old snow, blackened by road scum.

My therapist is enthusiastic, just out of graduate school. Her bare face glows with kindness and no makeup, just a spray of red freckles. Instantly, my maroon lipstick feels cartoonish, and my pregnant body feels gigantic, as if I am filling the entire frozen food aisle, ballooning into the freezer doors on both sides. It's not my therapist's fault, though—it's a complete coincidence that we are practically neighbors. That is to say, her parents live two doors down from me on Summit Avenue, and Sophie loves to visit their backyard during our walks because they still have a ramshackle wooden playhouse from when their own children, including my therapist, were small. In the Center City phonebook, my therapist is listed under her married name. How could I have known? Anyway, there aren't a lot of therapists in this town. I pull my cartoon lips closed across my teeth and arrange them into the shape of a smile before glancing at the many flavors of ice cream.

"I'm sorry," my therapist says. "Your privacy, I mean. I shouldn't have said hello. It just slipped out. We don't tell anyone who we see—we take that seriously, you know."

———

Sometimes, Sophie bites. Once, she got me right on the swollen, outie button of my pregnant belly. In the shower the next morning, I see it: a purple bruise in the shape of a half heart. Mostly Sophie bites at night, as we snuggle on my big bed and I tell rambling stories of the people on the watery isthmus. I make up the stories as I go, and if I should happen to pause, Sophie pleads, "More! More!" So, I keep diving deeper for flotsam, opening my eyes underwater, searching the murky lake bottom for artifacts, a tiny saddle made of tooled leather, waterlogged songbooks belonging to the long-lost sister, an abandoned rowboat filled with soggy feathers. Inevitably, my eyelids begin to flutter and my sentences trail into the delicious borderlands between sleeping and waking. It happens so fast! The way she drops her little jaw, clamps down, razors those pointy new teeth into my arm, my shoulder, my hand. Once, she draws a spot of blood.

"She's not even two," John says when I tell him I'm afraid this biting thing is my fault, that I've done something to cause it. "Nah, she'll outgrow it," John says. "They always do."

"But you don't understand," I sob. "The books say biting is *serious*. I have to teach her to stop and I don't know how."

———

From her highchair, Sophie stares through the kitchen window, transfixed by two squirrels chasing each other around the huge trunk of our towering black walnut tree, a tree I love fiercely in spite of the colossal mess it makes each fall when the walnuts soften and rot, leaving their tarry juices to stain our yard and stick to our bare feet. Sophie has named the squirrels Carl and Sugar after her beloved *Good Dog, Carl* book, and after her favorite restricted food.

"Carl! Sugar!" Sophie shouts happily whenever she sees a squirrel outside, as if Carl and Sugar are the only two squirrels in the world. As if they are her very own squirrels, while also being entirely interchangeable with one another—and all other squirrels, for that matter. Just blurry bodies, running. Which they are, I suppose. Like all of us.

It takes so long to become anything. Especially yourself. I have stopped attending the incest survivors' group because of the moaning woman. I am too ashamed to tell my therapist about my aversion to the moaner, so I lie. I say my teenage babysitter has moved and I haven't found a replacement for those evenings. My therapist's office is in a modern building edged with crabgrass and thistle, now visible in the softening mud. This location serves as an outpost for the county clinic. The engraved plaque at the rear entrance still reads Haverland Dental, from back before Dr. Haverland moved to Chicago.

I tell my therapist about Sophie's biting. "Toddlers test you," she says. "You have to say no."

"I *do*. But I don't want to be harsh or scary. Like—"

"You're not your mother," my therapist says. "Being serious isn't the same as being mean. If Sophie ran into the street and you said no, would she stop?"

"I think so?"

"You need to *know* so. Just say no like you mean it." My therapist switches gears suddenly. "How is it between you and John?" she says. "Sexually, I mean."

"Well," I say. I tell her about the Nazi dreams. "They're not always Nazis, though. Sometimes they're robbers. Sometimes that guy from the movie *Halloween*. Sometimes—this is the weirdest—it's a jackalope, a bad one, sitting on my chest. No matter what it is, I'm half awake and can barely breathe or move."

Her left eyebrow shoots up, but only a little. "What do you do in the dream?" she says.

"Try to run," I say. "But I can't, and even if I can, there's always some kind of wall or cliff. I try to hide, but there's never any good hiding places. I end up crouching behind a chain-link fence or folding myself into a cardboard box or something like that while the enemy keeps coming for me."

"Then what?"

"I wake up."

Here's another reason I found a therapist: I read an article recently about how memories are stored in our cells. How every cell in the body is a holding tank for everything that's ever been, a microcosm of our entire life, packed into the dark recesses of our physical selves. Mafia had a silver scar on his nose from the time he got too rough with our little dog, Pete. He smelled like oil from his job at Exxon—oil and something else, musty and chemical. Once, he took my sister and me to Dairy Queen—and, instead of ordering kid cones for us the way Mom would have, he told us we could order whatever we wanted. I got a Peanut Buster Parfait.

The article said cellular memories are passed along from one generation to the next. It's called intergenerational trauma. This means Mafia is not only inside me, but also inside Sophie. He's in the new baby too, this creature not yet born, this creature who is, here in my therapist's office, jamming a sharp, miniature foot under my middle ribs. I didn't know about cellular memories before I decided, recklessly, to allow babies into my body. When I'm fiery and floating, I watch myself from above. My body is not me. I am the part that burns. About a third of every human body is made up of nonhuman matter—bacteria and noncellular material like bone and connective tissue. I am connected to my body by a string.

My therapist recommends books and articles about female sexuality, the art of foreplay, the common needs women have for arousal and orgasm—things I don't need to hear, because I don't care.

"How can you be sure, if you've never gotten what you need?" my therapist says. "You've been with—what, two other men?"

"Three."

"Okay, three. Remember, most women need to be touched."

"John isn't much of a toucher. But it's usually quick."

My therapist rests her chin on her fists and sighs. She continues speaking and speaking and speaking.

"Wait, it takes some women more than twenty minutes?" I ask, stunned, at the end of this frustrating but fascinating session.

———

I grow my first garden from seed. I have never grown anything before. Well, babies, but that's different. Anyway, I know the flowers will grow slowly. What I don't know is that the weeds will grow so much faster, exploding into a dense thicket that threatens to choke my flowers out.

"Nature takes over, doesn't she?" our neighbor Donna says whenever she eyes me between our houses, bent over my giant belly full of baby, staring into the tangled disaster of my would-be garden. I shrug and pretend to laugh. Donna doesn't look at me directly on these occasions. She just repeats her same tired line about nature, all stiff and what have you, from where she stands between her perfectly stick-straight garden rows with that fancy watering hose suspended in her green-gloved hand. Once, that orange cat of hers—which, incidentally, prowls our yard at will—scratched Sophie's perfect arm for no reason, just because Sophie loves cats and tried to pet him. Donna blamed Sophie.

I don't remember the names of the flowers I planted. I chose the seed packets for the colors—yellows and oranges with a few prettier reds and pinks. Plus, for Sophie, a smattering of purples because "the lost sister loved purple," she tells me.

———

"My garden is a wreck," I say to John as June folds into July. I am eight months pregnant. My body is two whole bodies, neither of which belongs to me.

"I could dig it up for you. Just say the word." John laughs as he says this, but not his real laugh—the barking one I don't like. Still, he's trying to be helpful, which I do like. It endears him to me. "Then you could start over next year," he says from the stove, where he is scrambling eggs for a breakfast-style dinner on an ordinary Thursday evening. Lately, in the dark of our bed, with John inside me—well, it's Mafia I'm talking about now, the oiliness of him. That's when I float up to the ceiling. It's not John's fault. He's a wonderful father. I was only two when my real father left—I called him Jack Daddy, because his name was Jack. Mafia was Daddy because Mom said so.

"I'd much rather weed the garden I already planted," I say to John. He's scooping scrambled eggs onto plates, dropping some onto the wood floor. He picks up those bits and puts them back onto the plates.

"Five-second rule," he says.

"But the whole thing is such a mess," I say. "Everything is all snarled together. I can't tell the weeds from the flowers."

"Just pull up the ugly stuff," John says through a mouthful of egg. "And leave the rest."

———

On the last day of July, Mom visits. She settles herself at our kitchen table, the one John and I bought at Target for our first apartment back in Minneapolis: slab of cheap pine, soft and light, now full of lines and divots from three years of scraping plates across it and chopping vegetables on it and pressing pens and pencils into it while writing checks and letters and grocery lists. In one spot, the table has the word *HURRY* etched from an incident during my maternity leave, before I quit my advertising-sales job at the newsweekly in Minneapolis. I was on the kitchen phone that day with my boss while also nursing Sophie, who spewed a ferocious stream of breastmilk across my chest and lap, soaking herself and me, and I needed John to grab towels, and fast. I should have just ended the call, of course. Called back after cleaning up the mess. But in those first, fragile days of motherhood, I still believed I could hide the dirt and indignity, the fluids and the bruised organs. I still believed I could hide anything at all.

"Uh-oh!" I say now, grabbing a green plastic letter *I* from Sophie, who is stuffing it into her mouth. I stick the magnet high on the refrigerator door. "Must have fallen off," I say to Mom. Mom wears her hair very short now, in grassy tufts much like those shag cuts she gave me as a child. She keeps tucking clumps behind her ears, between sips of the strong coffee I brewed for her. I drink cold raspberry leaf tea from a Mason jar. This concoction is meant to make labor easier, a tidbit I learned from one of my books on natural childbearing. A quart a day of this tea, I drink.

Mom's latest apartment is a tall, narrow duplex in the same Northeast neighborhood where John grew up. Her visit today is a rarity. Mom doesn't like highway driving, and Center City is almost an hour from Minneapolis, all highway. Normally, if I want Sophie to see Mom, I have to drive to wherever Mom is. Her new duplex situation makes visiting easier. The rooming house before the duplex was too awkward. Before the rooming house, well, those were the lost years, right after I aged out of the foster homes Rachael and I landed in when Mom lost the house. I didn't keep track of Mom during the lost years, so it surprised me after Sophie was born, it truly did, the balloon of yearning that rose in me. It filled the open cavity where Sophie had just been, expanded into an ache so deep it felt almost like pleasure. And why shouldn't I want my mama back? With me being an adult now, she doesn't have to *do* anything. Plus, with Sophie, maybe I can give her something she's never had—like the chance to love a child in the kind of uncomplicated way she could never love me.

"Isn't this house amazing, Mom?" I say. Mom glances around the old kitchen. Like the rest of the house, the kitchen is timeworn but charming—a vintage porcelain sink complete with drainboards, rough-hewn cupboards I painted white myself, light maple floor, and best of all, the wooden screen door to the porch overlooking the open water of North Center Lake. "Isn't it wonderful, Mom?"

Mom bends her grassy head over her coffee cup and sips. This is a thing Mom does, this silence when I try to goad her into praise. I want her to be proud of me for what I have accomplished: a marriage and family, my galloping mare of a daughter who already speaks extraordinary sentences, five and six words long and more, such as, *I do remember furry clouds!* And *Look, Mama! Tree arms in the sky!* I want Mom to notice how careful I am with Sophie, how when she bites me I never slap her mouth or even shout. Rather, I say, "Sophie, no biting," then lift her onto my lap and hold her. Only if she bites again, which she sometimes does, do I set her down more firmly and walk away to keep from losing my temper. And even on those few times when I have lost my temper and raised my voice, yelled that biting is *not okay,* is *bad,* and pulled Sophie off of me too roughly, yanked her doughy arm too hard, tried to hurt her *just a little,* I didn't mean it, not at all, and I won't ever defend myself for those times, not even to myself. I am *sorry,* so sorry that I've had to sit down from the way the room started to spin, from the way my chest seized up and forced the air from my lungs. I've had to fold myself in half, head to thighs, and breathe slowly until I could feel my whole body again in spite of the burning. Only then could I try once more to trust that I am always safe with Sophie and will never, ever hurt her.

"Mom?" I say again. "Isn't it something? This house?"

"House, mouse, louse," Mom says. "It's fine. It reminds me of Florence's old place in Duluth. Hers was smaller, of course. And not on the lake. Now she's up on the Iron Range."

"Interesting," I say, with no interest. I haven't seen or heard from my great aunt Florence since we left Duluth for Wyoming. I don't care. "How about Mafia?" I say meanly. "Is he still in the workhouse?" Tina, the daughter of the woman Mafia married after

Mom, reported Mafia a couple of years back for sexual misconduct. Apparently, Tina told a school counselor what Mafia was doing to her—had been doing for years, by then. Just as he had done to me. The counselor was mandated to tell social services, and she did. Tina's mom not only left Mafia immediately, but also, I can't help but note, did everything possible to make sure charges were pressed. That's why Mafia's a convicted sex felon now. "I wonder if he's on one of those neighborhood watch lists," I say. "Or post-office signs."

"I have no business tracking the doings of Maf—of Michael S_____," Mom says. "Nor do you."

"He molested me, Mom. That's a reason." This is not the conversation I planned. Nor is it one my mother and I have ever had, not even at the end of eighth grade after I saw that film about incest in health class, the one that prompted me to tell Mom what I remembered about Mafia. My announcement, back then, only tuned the thin string of silence between us to a sharper pitch. Here in my own kitchen, though, my Mason jar of herbal tea feels smooth and cool between my palms. It feels like the words *here* and *mine.* I watch myself wind up. I hear myself swing. "I hope he *is* still in the workhouse," I say. "I'm glad Tina's mother pressed charges, or whatever. It's crazy how—"

"It's shit and biscuits is what it is," Mom blurts out. A little moan gurgles out of her then, like the woman at the meeting, the woman I hate.

"What, Mom?" I say. Across the room, Sophie babbles cheerfully about *bigger, bigger, yellow, small* as she pulls old plastic bowls and aluminum pans from the bottom cupboard, which I have filled with these items just for her. Suddenly, she feels far away.

"I exerted myself, is what I'm saying," Mom says. "I made him go to counseling."

"For what? Counseling for what?"

"For the things he was—look, you know what for." She licks

the rim of her coffee cup, and the sight of her coated tongue fills my mouth with sand. I want to slap her.

"You're saying you knew, when I was little? You knew back then what he was doing, before I told you?" July sun bounces off the smooth surface of North Center Lake and pours brilliant white light into the room. Sophie's thin baby hair has sprung into sweaty ringlets, and her skin shines pink with summer. But I am shivering. Sophie looks up at me suddenly, her bright round face stretching open like a field toward a distant horizon, much farther away than I can see.

"I'm saying I was worried he might be, might have—and he said, he promised that after that he wouldn't," Mom says. "He promised it was over. Still, when he left that time, left Meadowlark Hills, after he smashed the furniture and whatnot, I said he had to get help. I said he had to, or he couldn't come back." Her lazy eye goes loose, while her strong eye, aimed dead on me, narrows and hardens. I picture her as a child on the farm in Smithville, with her eye patch and Coke-bottle glasses. I picture her playing in the forbidden woods behind the old tracks, tripping and crashing down on that rusty railroad spike, a perfect arc of blood pulsing from her thigh.

"Mom," I say. The sound of my own voice is amplified in my ears, as if traveling through deep water. "I was barely older than Sophie." My throat swells shut around these shards of language.

Mom pushes herself up from the table and carries her coffee cup to the sideboard of that farmhouse sink I love so much. She leans against the porcelain, her broad back to me. From behind, Mom's hair is both flattened and tufting sideways. It hurts to look at her. I scoop Sophie up and balance her little body around my waist, her plump legs encircling the mound of my pregnant belly. I edge toward the porch door. Mom spins around and claps her hands, once, twice, three times. "Jeannie," she says. "I am now closing the book on Michael S_____ and this particular sorrow. I recommend you do the same. Every day, women are raped and beaten. They get over it. And so should you. Until then, do not darken my door with your self-pity."

My mother turns back around to face the sink again, rinses her cup under the faucet, sets it exactly where it was a moment before, then slings her purse over her shoulder. I imagine the silver pin under her skin from the surgery she had after the explosion she survived when she was a new mother; I picture the way the twisted metal keeps her arm stuck to her body as she walks through the narrow hallway, past the steep basement stairs, through the mudroom, and out my back door, her shadow stretching out long before her.

Sophie cranes her neck in my mother's direction, uncurls her starfish hand to wiggle her fingers slowly at the empty spot where her grandmother just was. "Grandma bye-bye?" she says.

———

I have a sea of rage in me. Also, a baby. I can reconcile neither.

My mother is an old forty-four. To me, she is already dried up and sexless. A crone, like in the fairy tales I read to Sophie. Who believes anymore that a crone can be a fairy in disguise? I would like to see this magic. But maybe a crone is just a crone. I don't ever want to be one. But I'm also afraid that in some fundamental way, I already am one, and always will be.

Here's what Mom says about her own mother, Grandma Krause, who died before I was born. She says Grandma Krause wanted my mother to be a boy and expected this to be the case, considering how low she was carrying. "Any lower and I'd be dragging this child on the sidewalk," Grandma Krause liked to say in her last agonizing weeks of pregnancy. When, instead of a boy, my mother squawked into the world, Grandma Krause was shocked. To console herself, she named my mother Georganne and called her George, the same name she had planned for the son who didn't come. George, the name of my mother's father and grandfather.

My mother's Smithville home was a squat clapboard farmhouse in a field on the edges of Duluth. I never asked if the chickens that lived upstairs in winter had dominion over the whole second floor. Mom only talked about the squawking and the shit. Details make the legend, and the legend forms its own truth. Another legend—though this could be wrong, too—is how once during an overnight bender, Mom's uncles burned down the outhouse. When she trudged across the sopping grass the next morning, all she found to piss in was a hole in the ground and a pile of smoking ash. What I know for sure, though, is that Grandma and Grandpa Krause were both dead by the time Mom turned seventeen, the same year she got pregnant and married my father.

Then the party on Park Point.

Here's how I imagine that thick summer night. Mom was eighteen and smoking True Blues, her teased hair sprayed stiff, Coral Candy lipstick to match her dress. My father was a young James Dean, what with his tight Levi's and leather jacket, hair slicked back with Brylcreem. As for me, I was up the hill in the West End at Aunt Flossie's—Mom had roped her younger sister into babysitting. I was probably asleep. Maybe crying. Maybe gazing at Flossie with my watery newborn eyes, wise and floating. I was still easy then.

Park Point is a narrow, seven-mile sand spit across the metal lift bridge from Duluth's working harbor. Stretching south from the port of Duluth, the point divides the mean waters of Lake Superior from Superior Bay and the Duluth Harbor Basin. Later my mother would tell me how the beach shack shook that night as bodies packed in by the dozen, everyone smoking and drinking and shouting over each other and over the songs that poured from the record player—"Hey Jude" and "Mrs. Robinson" and "Sunshine of Your Love." Fumes from the hardboard-processing plant across the bay filled the air. High above the lake, a flat disc of moon hung like a nickel, slicing open the black water with a sharp tunnel of light. In the house, faces shone and T-shirts clung damp across chests and under arms. Mom sat on the green brocade couch in the postage-stamp living room, her long legs crossed at the knee, the last of her cigarette in one hand, a warm beer in the other, her two best friends on either side of her also smoking and drinking.

Mom's cheeks, round and high, glowed with alcohol and summer. Glowed with sex. But her lazy eye went loose—the patch she'd worn as a child for her amblyopia had never corrected the problem entirely—as she watched her young husband holding court in the harvest gold of the kitchen. He was telling his best story, Mom could see, the one about his motorcycle accident on Skyline Parkway. It was obvious in the way he gestured with his arms and his hands, indicating the road ahead, indicating the rain, the oncoming car. It was also evident in how the women's lips parted, how their eyes softened with want. Mom clenched her jaw. But wait: he *had* married her, hadn't he? She sucked in her stomach, still fleshy from me, and yanked at her thick bra straps to hoist up her breasts, hard as rocks and hot with milk. *Christ, though.* She wanted more.

The friend on Mom's right side leaned in and pointed toward my father, whispered something pungent with beer and tobacco. Mom threw her head back and laughed. She tapped her cigarette and watched the long, soft snake of ash fall to the floor.

Then: an enormous hollow boom and blinding light. Bodies and furniture rose weightlessly above the ball of fire as windows blew out and the walls of the shack collapsed in four directions, falling out like playing cards. The pitched roof billowed up fifty feet closer to the moon before crashing to the ground again.

A gas line had busted under the floorboards.

Mom's two best friends died instantly, while Mom was thrown a dozen feet from the house before landing like a cloth doll on the dirt, shoulder ripped from socket, ear dangling from scalp. *We thought she had died,* Aunt Flossie always said. *Too many people jumping up and down,* is how Mom always told it. *She flicked a cigarette,* my dad continued to say so many years later that it seemed cruel, really, to blame Mom still.

Several people were killed in that explosion. As the house burned, flashing lights flooded the sandbar in red and blue, sirens howled across the water as squads and fire trucks and ambulances rushed to find the house already reduced to blackened sticks.

My father, unhurt, watched it smolder.

The brain is an extremely fragile organ. It is made up of delicate soft tissue that floats inside the skull. The severity and permanence of injury to the brain depend on the degree or extent of damage. Specific scale scores should always be used to measure damage to the brain in order to determine the right treatment. Treatment should begin as soon as possible and continue as long as necessary. *Should* is a slippery word. My mother's ear was sewed back on. Her shoulder was pinned together. That is all we know.

———

I march out the porch door and into my side garden. Sophie marches behind me, dragging her blanket in one hand and my ratty childhood doll, Burnett, in the other. I named Burnett when I was four, after my favorite TV star, Carol Burnett. At first, I called the doll Carol, but my cousin said that was too boring. Now, Sophie mothers Burnett with a ferocious brand of love, as if seeking to reform a defiant new recruit. It's comical, really, the strictness of Sophie's doll discipline, when I myself struggle with setting any limits at all. "No, no, no!" Sophie yells. "Do not touch!" While Sophie instructs Burnett, I bend over as best I can to pull, claw, yank, and tear at all the ugly stuff I can find. It's demanding work, and at some point, I begin to groan. Sophie stops mid-tirade. "Mama owie?" she says, her face clouding with worry.

"No, honey," I say. "Mama's just weeding."

Sophie resumes her scolding. "No biting!" she says to Burnett. Then, in a conspiratorial whisper, "I bite Mama."

When Sophie eventually fusses, I ferry her back inside, where John is making dinner—a congee recipe he grew fond of when his mother hosted a Korean nun years ago. John eats his congee with kimchi. I can barely eat mine plain. This pregnancy has been relentless with its nausea, not to mention the deep, painful eruptions along my jawline. Something about the hormones. Sophie has gathered her macaroni noodles with butter and peas into a little mountain on the tray of her highchair. She babbles on about some imagined conflict between Carl and Sugar. "Carl do it first," she says. "Now kiss Sugar. Say sorry."

After dinner, I bathe Sophie and, after jammies and tooth brushing, tell her another story of the isthmus people—this time, about a good witch who lives in a house tucked so neatly behind another house that we have never even noticed it. "And that house is frozen," I say, tucking Sophie's ringlets behind her ear, tracing the soft hollow of her temple. "It's covered in icicles always, even in summertime. And because of the way the ice sparkles, and because the house is so close to the water, it looks like a diamond, just floating away on the lake." Blessedly, Sophie falls asleep before I do—no biting at all—and I go straight back to my garden. The sky is not yet dark, but the moon dangles high above the lake, a small, bright thing, barely half of itself. It is either—what is that called?—waxing or waning. Wax on, wax off. I have no idea. This garden too is half of what it was before I began weeding—yet it is also somehow more, I think, as my pile of ripped-up quack grass and dandelions grows satisfyingly large.

Apparently, some weeds are obvious, even to me. Mom was orphaned at seventeen. Chickens lived in her house. Mafia beat her in front of me. These are facts, but I don't know what they mean to me or to my cells. *Cognition* refers to thinking, but thought takes many forms. Before I dropped out of college, I took two years of Latin. In that language, *cognoscere* means not only to know but to learn, inquire, experience. I drop to my knees and tear harder, wrenching at whatever I find, ropy stems and prickly leaves. I attack the overgrowth until my palms blister, my back and hips ache, my knees carve divots into the ground. This work is addictive, a trance of never-ending elimination.

Demolition is like that. It sucks you in. It swallows.

By the time I rise to assess the emptiness I've carved, I recognize the tight pain between my hips and my ribs as more than gardening. This baby is on its way.

"Should I call my mom?" John says when I come inside.

"Not yet," I say. "Wait till I'm good and close."

———

"Guess what sweetie? You're almost there!" This is what the nurse says when she examines me on arrival. Her hands are warm and gentle. "Just a skip and a jump, hon." She pats my shoulder and grins. I think I'm not a very good feminist for liking how she calls me *sweetie* and *hon,* but I do like it, very much. Soon after the nurse completes her exam, she is at the door. "Hit the buzzer when things pick up," she says as she leaves. John feeds me ice chips as I ride cascading waves of pain. This homey country birthing room is a far cry from the high-tech city hospital where Sophie was born, where I was hooked up to a monitor and Pitocin, where a male doctor I'd never met sliced me open wide to make pushing go faster. I am happy here in this sleepy, low-lit place, laboring in my own way, with my raspberry leaf tea and some black cohosh to speed things along.

Before dawn, my water breaks with a gush. I vomit.

"Atta girl!" John says happily. He remembers this turning point from Sophie's birth. He laughs, his real laugh. We whisper together between contractions until it comes, the fiercest wave yet. Here is the nurse again. Now the doctor. My body seizes and rolls through the shocks that follow, and I stare into the void behind my closed eyes, entranced by what I see. Giant weeds coming up through the darkness, one after the next, rhythmic and ghostly, white roots intact, wet dirt clinging to fine-haired tendrils. "Visualize your cervix opening, the baby moving through you," the nurse says. I try then to think of Jackson Street, those roses opening petal by petal. I try and I try, but in this long, dark tunnel where I float, weightless and dizzy, I see only weeds, weeds pulled up by the root, one after the other after the other, until something else finally pulses its way through the darkness too, something fiery, something that burns and slides back into myself. This is my body, filling my body. Into this vision—weeds drawn from fertile soil over and over again, weeds and the rich, heady smell of dirt, weeds and the awkward act of pulling life from life, life into life, one thing to die and another to live—my son is born.

This boy is neither flower nor weed. He doesn't come from the earth. He comes from me. The part that burns is the part that glows. My body is bigger than my body. My body is a nebula, hydrogen and helium, dust and plasma. Bodies are made of cells, cells are made of atoms, and atoms are billions of years old. My son is slick against my naked chest. His skin is the exact same temperature as mine. His tiny bones are soft and alive. His mouth is a mouth, searching for home—and home is the stellar nursery of my skin, my breath, my milk. "Hello, baby," I say. His gray eyes float through light-years to fix on mine. This, I realize, is a covenant.

"Waning moon," John says, pointing out the hospital window. So, now I know. But it doesn't matter because soon enough, the moon will wax again. But not everything that leaves comes back. I don't know what will become of my mother, or the woman who moans, or me, or John, or Mafia, or any of us. I think of Carl and Sugar, their blurry, anonymous squirrel bodies, always running. I still don't know what it means. Here's what I do know: I am a moon, and Sophie fits in my hollows, no matter the shape I take, and so too must my son. "Look at you," I whisper. His name will be Maxwell, for deep water.

"You need to push, hon," the nurse says. The placenta is still inside of me, and I have to push it out now, this temporary organ formed from the same bundle of cells that also became this tiny creature, the one in my arms, studying my face like a familiar constellation. In some cultures, the placenta is called the twin. In this rural hospital, it is just a placenta. Still, I will be allowed to take it home in a plastic ice cream bucket, and I will bury it in my garden, where the placenta will decompose into simple matter to begin again. Scientists say our cells hold everything forever. But, also, cells are constantly dying and regenerating. Sometimes cellular regeneration hurts, but not always. Scientists say the body replaces itself with an almost entirely new set of cells every seven to ten years. Some important parts are renewed even faster. Other important parts are never renewed. All these facts are true.

"Push," the nurse says again. "You have to push." She presses hard on my stomach with one hand—a graphic kind of pain—and strokes my forehead with the other, which makes me cry. "You can do this," she says. "Just push!"

And so I do. I push.

9th Grade English, Unit One: Autobiography

I was born April 9, 1968, a warm spring day. My mother left for St. Mary's Hospital in Duluth, Minnesota, around five o'clock in the morning and at 9:55, I opened my eyes to see Leon D. Kohn, who delivered me. I weighed seven pounds, ten ounces, and measured twenty-one inches. My nurse put a tiny ribbon in my hair for a special touch.

I was an agreeable baby with lots of smiles and laughs and a good appetite. I enjoyed attention, and devised several little tricks to attract it. Unlike many babies, I slept like a log all night, endearing myself to my parents. I realize what a gift it must have been to have a baby who didn't cry all night, because, later, my younger sister would keep the whole family awake many times with her un-silenceable screams. My mother did a wonderful job recording many of these details in my baby book. A photo in the book shows me sitting on my mother's stomach as she reclines on a couch. I have many fond memories, some of my fondest, in fact, of sitting this way with my mother and practicing my numbers as a small child.

First Christmas

At my first Christmas, I was only nine months old. More fascinating to me than the glorious tree, merry festivities, and countless gifts, was my beautiful dress with a real hooped skirt. Photos show me having some difficulty controlling that hoop. Nevertheless, I was thrilled by it. All through my childhood, nothing pleased me more than a dress or skirt with lots of ruffles that could spin and flare out. All in all, my first Christmas was a very, very happy one for everyone.

First Birthday

I have always been a great lover of parties. For that reason and more, my first birthday means so much to me now. I was unfortunately quite a little slob when it came to the cake, but I nonetheless had a wonderful time. I realized right then and there that birthdays are special occasions full of memories to be cherished forever.

When I Was One

I have a stubborn streak that obviously developed at a very early age. As my mother wrote in my baby book under One Year Old, "Well, Jeannie, you are still a beast!" Whenever I set my mind to do something, I did it, and that was that. At one year old, I was able to go up and down stairs, ride a toddler's bike, swing on a swing, climb a ladder, slide down a slide, and ride a teeter totter with my mother. *Captain Kangaroo* and *Romper Room* were my favorite television programs. One problem I had was a strong attachment to my pacifier. As a matter of fact, if my mother even spelled out the letters "P-A-C-I-F," I knew what she was referring to and would either cry for it, or, if I already had it, show it to her.

When I Was Two

Being two is wonderful for a two-year-old, but having a two-year-old can be murder for a parent. Luckily for my parents, I was a happy, cheerful child, full of singing and dancing. I made numerous friends in the neighborhood. I loved to play house, especially if I was the mama, since I had a passionate love for babies, which I still possess. My mother considered me too brave for my own good after I took a ride down a hill on a toboggan and loved it, crying for more. I was an out-of-doors person and could play until I was completely exhausted. When it came to taking walks, however, I preferred the stroller. My imagination was always very active, and I had a flair for making up stories at will. Much to my mother's dismay, I was an unreasonably picky eater, and would go on streaks where I would refuse all but one kind of food for weeks at a time. Any kind of candy or dessert, however, always appealed to my appetite, and I still have an uncontrollable sweet tooth.

By two, I had mastered the feats of washing my face and hands and putting on my own shoes. I was working on dressing myself as well. I also loved to play with blocks and would build things for hours on end. All in all, I wasn't too terrible when I was two, because I saved that for when I as three, as you will soon see.

With this, I end my introduction and begin a series of descriptions of important events that made my childhood unique to me, and a childhood worth preserving in my memory forever. However, since I have made many, many moves in my life, please do not become confused when the location of my story changes rapidly and without explanation.

Playing Pool

I had many great adventures when I was three, which I still remember quite vividly today. One of those adventures took place as I was playing with my friend Jerry. Jerry and I were great buddies, and we often played in my back yard. On the day in question, Jerry and I wandered together into my neighbor's yard and discovered her basement door ajar. Our natural curiosity led us through the door and down the stairs. Much to our delight, we found a fuzzy green table with wonderful colored balls all over it. Somehow, we managed to get every last ball down from that table. We then hauled the balls up the stairs to the yard, where we proceeded to load them into my trusty red wagon and drag them to the sidewalk. Can you guess what we did next? Right! We rolled them down the hill and watched them go in colorful streaks. On our way back home, Jerry ran in front of me and was therefore caught red-handed by his mother who saw that he still had one red pool ball in his hands.

He could not deny it. As for me, I saw trouble ahead, and did what anyone would do. I hid.

Tot

I have not yet mentioned my great aunt Tot in this autobiography, but my mother has always told many fascinating stories about her. Now I will tell a story of my own. It happened when I was three or four, and I recall exactly how the accident took place. I was visiting my Uncle Orville and Aunt Betty, my cousins, and Tot, who loved to give me money in the form of coins. This time, Tot gave me several pennies, and, out of habit, I popped one into my mouth. Tot quickly warned me not to do this, but I, of course, believed it was a perfectly safe practice.

My belief was dead wrong. Not long after Tot left the room, the penny slid into the back of my mouth. I was panic stricken, but remained brave. I tried to cough the penny up, but could not. I tried to fish the penny out with my finger. This, also, proved impossible. My only choice was to swallow the penny, which by now was lodged deep in my throat. Then, the penny worked its way painfully down my small esophagus. Once settled in my stomach, the penny created an ache so severe it was all I could do to keep from crying. I was also afraid of getting in trouble for putting the penny in my mouth. Therefore, I told no one.

With this incident, I will proceed to my school-age years, which have brought me great joy and challenge, and provided the opportunity to meet many new people and make many new friends.

Pete

When he was small enough to fit in my hand, my dog Pete was brought to our door in Duluth by a man who said, "I found him in the street. If he's not yours, I'll put him back." Needless to say, my mother claimed him. Now, he lives with family friends in Iowa, because no pets are allowed in our apartment.

Head Start

At four years old, I entered Head Start at Bryant School in Duluth. I have few outstanding memories of this experience other than a particular dress, one my mother sewed for me, that I adored. It was blue and white checkered with a ruffled pinafore. After Head Start, kindergarten and first grade flew by. Then my family moved from Duluth to Douglas, Wyoming. By this time, I had a baby sister, Rachael, who was fathered by my mother's second husband. I was excited and thrilled by the move to Wyoming, but Rachael was too young to remember it. We did not stay in Douglas long. In the middle of my second-grade year, we moved to Casper, Wyoming. I loved each and every one of these moves, although I did regret leaving the many, many friends I would inevitably make at each new school. I have gone to nine different schools so far.

Wyoming

Wyoming was my home for six extremely happy years. I attended grades two through six in three different elementary schools and I loved them all. Sixth grade, especially, was magical from start to finish and I will cherish my sixth-grade memories forever.

After sixth grade, my mother moved us to Minneapolis so that I could spend more time with my father, while still having my mother nearby. I have always had a special love for my father. Even though my parents divorced when I was two years old, my father and I have remained exceptionally close. During seventh and eighth grade, I lived with my father and his wife and their new children. Many good things came of those two years, one of them being the close relationship I established with my four-year-old sister, Janie. She looks exactly like I did when I was four.

As for my father, he is thinking about moving to Florida sometime in the near future. He owns moped shops, so living in Florida would increase his business due to the all-year moped-riding season which is found there.

Life in 1982

This brings me to the present. I am currently attending Alexander Ramsey High School, and enjoying every minute of it (almost). My favorite class is Spanish. I love to read, and recently finished *The Count of Monte Cristo*. It was an excellent book about a prisoner who escapes and transforms himself, and I enjoyed it tremendously.

Wingless Bodies

I. Void

My father is not a swan. His bones are not hollow inside his flesh. The spaces between the phalanges of his feet are not spanned by delicate black webbing.

My father has never once trumpeted.

My father has no air sacs on his lungs. The doctors would have seen these when they cut through his not-hollow breastbone to expose and unblock his heart. The idea is, use an open artery to make a new pathway. The conclusion is, close the original wound.

My father's chest was pried open in Florida—who knows how many curves of the river from Minnesota, where I stood with the phone in my hand as he lay on the table. Minnesota, where my father was born and my mother was born and I was born with weak lungs and a spine that grew crooked toward the window.

Florida is far from the saltless amniotic waves of Lake Superior, far from the sulfur and stench and seduction of this river that flows through our bodies toward the sea, toward the Gulf of Mexico, where my father lives, recklessly, without air sacs.

Air sacs and hollow bones are like life preservers. They keep swans afloat. I have never seen my father float. Partly this is because he does not care for water. Partly it is because I have so rarely seen my father, who, unlike a swan, did not mate for life.

II. Source

The Mississippi gurgles up from a clumsy knob-and-kettle landscape. Knobs are hills filled with coarse gravel and boulders dropped like loose change by the glacier's edge. Kettles are scars filled in by melt water to make lakes and ponds and bogs.

At the headwaters, I was seventeen when Cyrus fucked me in a damp tent. I watched from above, recalling my stepfather's coarse hands. I bled, but it didn't hurt. It hurt, but it wasn't Cyrus's fault. It was his fault, but he was scarred. And I was scarred. And melt water runs downhill. We could have had the baby, but we didn't. Cyrus stole stuff and sold it. Cars, drugs, guns, and something else, like that small thing inside him that was naked and open-beaked. Cyrus went to prison.

The headwaters are best crossed holding a child's hand. Sometimes this threshold is no more than a rivulet you can skip over. The dust on your feet stays dry. Other times the only way is to crawl in and lie down. Let the water rush over your supine body. Let the river run into your open mouth. Maybe you pull yourself out.

I got married. I had babies. I brought them, wild and un-combed, to the source, where they scratched notes in careful cursive: *This is the message. We are at the top of the river. Who are you? Please put us back in the water. We are floating to the sea.* Carefully, they burnt the edges of these scrolls, match after match. Then they launched them in glass bottles toward the Gulf, where the fresh water spills into the brine.

III. Dive

This river shapes my words, wears them down, spits them up onto the bank in piles of gravel and heaps of heavy round stones.

Sometimes it hurts.

I never learned how to sing alone without looking over my shoulder. Not even in the shower. If you sing with me, though, I will find you. I will layer my voice on top of yours, inside of yours, like wax pooling in a candle, contained and alive in that column of light.

When babies cry, we sing. Our voices pull anguish into melody, float fear and sadness between layers of sound.

When the page before us is empty and untamed, we take it into our mouths. We chew it, fibrous and thick, until we can finally swallow it down.

My mom was eighteen and smoking True Blues when the house exploded. She was with my dad at a party, their newborn across town, maybe asleep. Gas line busted under the floorboards. Three girlfriends on the couch, two dead, my mom tossed from where she sat between them, a dozen feet into the yard, shoulder ripped from socket, ear dangling from scalp. We thought she had died, my aunt says. Too many people jumping up and down, my mom says. Someone flicked a cigarette, my dad says.

Enormous hollow boom of blinding light.

I was twenty-two when my first baby arrived, silent and awake. It was a cold August, and she was a perfect slippery thing, puckered and featherless yet bigger than me, bigger than all of us. Limitless. Somehow the walls did not buckle and fall, the floor and ceiling did not blow out, though she expanded everywhere, like sea, like sky. I will never forget how it felt to hold her, salty and oceanic, my firstborn daughter, who breathed under water, and who would teach me, finally, how to dive.

IV. Fire

As embryos, regeneration is our default state. We lose our knack for it, though, except for stray parts: arteries, skin, lungs, isolated regions of the brain. Only the liver and severed bits of fingertips can grow all the way back.

Even this could be a love story.

Burns are slow to heal, and can occur with or without flame.

"Help," I said to my husband, ten years into the blackening woods. "I can't breathe." A wildfire is a large, destructive blaze that spreads quickly over woodland or brush, as with divorce. "Not everyone needs to breathe," my husband said. Carefully, I struck a match. "Adulteress," my husband said. He summoned the God of Wind. Our children froze, the light reflected in their eyes. "Hide!" I said. "Watch it burn," he said. In the event that your hair or clothes catch fire, you must drop to the ground, cover your face, and roll to smother the flames. "It hurts," I said. Smoldering is a slow, low-temperature form of combustion, as with an aftermath.

Still, I love the smell of wood smoke and tobacco. I dream of the cigarettes I smoked in high school, butts tossed into the parking lot, into the river, out of the window of Eva's Ford Pinto, careening down Snelling Avenue, crazy with sun and Madonna's promise of a first touch. Later, hunched over a smoldering coffee can in the basement during the winter of the divorce.

A trillion cigarette butts end up as litter every year. How many were mine? How many still are?

My son is a certified wildfire fighter. "Most wildfires are arson," he tells me on a scorching July night, sharp hook of a moon dangling above. "Sometimes it's firefighters who do it," he says, "so they can earn money when fire season is slow." Fire starting is a felony. But workers need work. The air is hot and wet, alive with the smell of the river and the rising smoke of my son's Marlboro.

V. Horizon

The Arabic language has a word for love, *Ya'aburnee*. It means: you bury me.

This is Brighton Beach on Lake Superior. Today is his first time here, the man I was never supposed to love but will someday marry on this exact stretch of shattered volcanic rock, our kids lined up in a half circle. The air will be bright and filled with bees. Now, though, rain sheets sideways, like needles. Marathoners limp onto the beach, radiant and broken.

At the water's edge, we stand and stare into the mist. Mist forms when warm air meets low temperatures, as with breath exhaled into the cold.

"I see the horizon," he says.

"I don't," I say.

"I see us," he says. "I see our kids—yours, and mine. I see everything."

Mist creates a visible beam of light, refracting and reflecting from suspended droplets. When you see me, I exist. When you see all of me, all of me exists.

"I am not your father," he says years later, on a bad day.

"But you are," I say. "My father, my stepfather, my son. You are every man I have ever known. There is no other way."

"Okay," he says.

I have no taste for piles of small talk. The body knows what it knows, and skin remembers. I believe this man when he says he will outlive me so I can die in his arms. *This is a message.* Fire is not the only lick that scars. I want to burrow under the skin of this world and feel its bready heat. *I am at the top of the river.* I want to press my crooked backbone against the rocks. *Who are you?* I want his wingless body, his solid bones. The rest is feathers and ash. *Please put me back in the water.* I want the imperfect circle of our open mouths, melting like wax through the only artery.

We are, all of us, floating to the sea.

Open Water

The day I stop wanting to look out over open water begins like any other—an unusually brilliant morning in November, warm and cloudless, North Center Lake blinding under a cool sun. This time of year, the lake bounces so much light into our house that our whole kitchen burns with it. Until the lake skins over with ice, that is. John is making biscuits with mushroom gravy, his specialty. I am frying eggs. Cat Stevens is crooning "Oh Very Young," and John is singing along in his enthusiastically tuneless way while also trying to tell me something about work. "She said I'd make a great principal," he says between lines of the chorus—*something about denim blue and sky, something about lasting forever*—a kickass principal, is what she said."

"Who said?"

"Gretchen. My student teacher?"

"Hand me that metal spatula," I say. Max is on my hip—he's big for two, and heavy—and John is closer to the utensil crock. At the table, Sophie colors feverishly, then erases until she tears holes through the paper, flimsy as newsprint, that John pilfers from the middle school where he teaches. Sophie does not yet know how erasers can burn, leave scars. She narrates her scenes out loud: *Run, Carl, run!* and *Now you have wings! Fly, fly!* and *No biting, Sugar!* Thank God, she herself almost never bites anymore, although she does still talk about biting, with an air of what I can only describe as longing.

John hands me the spatula. "Of course, you'd make a great principal," I say. "Everyone knows that." It would suit John, too, being a principal, making big decisions—he's known for deciding things quickly and without hesitation. Adults make 35,000 decisions a day, he always says, and with each one, we become more depleted. It costs energy to belabor things. Trust your gut. John chooses his path and sets down it, rarely looking back. Like when he decided to be a teacher, or to call off his wedding to the first Janine. For John, decision and action are a single powerful gesture. It's beautiful, in its way, that immediacy, like an eagle airborne one moment, wings flattened against the blue of the sky, and nosediving the next, all muscle and downward force, plunging toward unbroken sea or undulating field, toward that single flicker of motion signaling the possibility of survival for another day.

John goes on about the in-service—interdisciplinary *blah*, *blah*, *blah*, he says, like how can they present these ideas as if they're new when the research has been clear for decades, and God, what pains in the asses student teachers can be, how lucky to get a competent one, not like that idiot in Sharon Green's room, the one who couldn't teach his way out of a paper bag, and, actually, last Monday, told a gaggle of seventh-grade girls that he was too hung over to help with their two-step algebraic word problems. John's teacher rants are familiar to me after five years of marriage, so it isn't until we're settled at the table, John and Sophie on one side, Max and me on the other, all of us breaking open our egg yolks and tearing apart steaming biscuits—the gravy is perfect—that I notice how every time John says her name, *Gretchen*, he smiles a tiny smile, just a flicker on the left side of his smooth upper lip—he never has been able to grow a mustache, though occasionally he tries—such a smooth lip, barely twitching.

I've met Gretchen on one of my trips to the school, bringing the kids to visit John's classroom. She's lovely. Straight dark hair all the way down her back, impossibly shiny. Young, of course, and those teeth. The same perfect white squares that the prettiest girls always have. John is still talking now, but his words run together, tangle themselves into a knot as Sophie asks for more gravy and Max knocks over his juice. By the time I've cleaned up the spill, the kids are basically finished. I scrape my mostly untouched eggs and biscuits into the trash. There is a kind of wind inside my body.

While John fills the old porcelain sink, I clear the table. John likes washing dishes. Another admirable trait. "Come on, guys," I say to the kids when the table is empty. "I have a surprise." Sophie grabs my old doll Burnett from the floor, plucks another biscuit from the platter, and gallops behind Max and me into the small wallpapered study on the far side of our dining room. I close the door of the study behind myself and kneel down on the oak floor in order to lean in very, very close to my children's eager, round faces. Those silken cheeks. "You know what Mama's going to let you do?" I say to them. "Watch a—" Before I can finish, Sophie is bucking and shrieking with joy, tiny biscuit bits flying from her mouth. Max shrieks too, and Sophie swings him around by his arms. "Maxie! Hop on!" she shouts. "Horsie will give you a ride!" I slide *The Red Balloon* into the VCR. The kids were enchanted by this film when we watched it recently for the first time. A film like this—well, it counts more as art than TV, I think. Plus, Max won't cry this time when Pascal loses his red balloon, because, having seen this film before, Max knows the ending, can look forward to the other balloons appearing en masse just in time to rescue the sad boy.

On my way back to the kitchen, I turn off Cat Stevens. Tuck my stupid, unwashed chin-length hair behind my stupid, unwashed ears. It's just John and me now in this November light. Just us and the rhythmic splashing of our neighbor, bailing water from his giant koi pond and tossing it onto the frozen grass. November is the season for emptying. Splash, splash, splash.

I sit at the table—the end with the word *HURRY* etched into the pine—and rest my chin on my knuckles. I sit this way for some time, until John finally turns around, flips up his palms toward the ceiling, like, *what? What?*

"Gretchen," I say.

"Gretchen?" John wipes the grease out of the cast iron pan with a paper towel. Never use soap and water on cast iron, he always says.

"Sit down," I say.

He does not sit down.

"Is there something going on?" I say.

John sets the pan on the table and gives me a long, straight look. His eyes are so beautiful. The deepest brown, and the exact same shape as Max's, those outer corners sloping always downward into a minor chord, even when he is happy, even when he is laughing. Cold radiates from my pelvis. Outside the kitchen window, two little girls—probably four years old, maybe five—stamp along the sidewalk in colorful plastic raincoats—one bright yellow and the other a mess of flowers. I watch them move in near silhouette, the lake blazing behind them.

"Okay," John says. He sits down. "Okay. I like her. I do. It was—you know, the way she looked at me, and I thought—so last week, I asked her out."

"You asked her *out?*" The neighbor's splashing has stopped, but now my pulse splashes through my ears, a torrent inside my head.

"I'm sorry." John touches my arm and I yank it back, pin it to my side. "Come on," he says. "I'm really sorry. That's why I told you."

"You didn't *tell* me. I *asked* you."

"But I was going to tell you. Listen, I didn't even do anything. I like her. Liked her, I mean. But that's it."

I stare past him to those little girls, dancing around on the sidewalk in their bright raincoats on this dry, windy day. John's voice does have sorrow in it, genuine sorrow. But it's obvious the sorrow is not for me. It is for him—for the pain of wanting and not getting. I want to scratch his face. Pull his hair.

"Get out," I whisper. "Just get out."

"Christ, Jeannie," he says. "Nothing happened. And she'll be gone next week, anyway. Their internships are over."

"You make me sick," I say. I'm sweating through my shirt, cold droplets rolling slowly from under my arms down my ribcage. It occurs to me with a jolt that I am very, very ugly. A monster, really. And old now, too? I am twenty-six, and already a crone. I am everything I have most feared becoming. And I don't care. I lean across the table, breathe heavily, hiss, "How dare you. How *dare* you? Here I am, taking care of our children day and night, while you're off falling in love with a twenty-year old."

"Twenty-five," John says. "Which is not the point, I know. It's just, when I gave her a ride to the in-service—"

"You gave her a ride to the fucking in-service?"

He turns up his palms again.

My throat swells, but I will not cry. Instead, I swallow hard, swallow again. Soft tissue tightens around my words and somehow serrates them, so they emerge as ragged strands of sound. "What did Gretchen say, exactly, when you asked her out?"

"I told you. She said no." John is pleading now. "She said, maybe you should talk to your wife."

———

There is more, though. More than a single bright Sunday in November, one pretty student teacher with impossibly smooth hair and a wide smile. What happened before that day was how I came apart after Max was born, how the pieces of me pulled away from each other like poorly laid sod on parched Wyoming soil. Even as I put myself back together, those pieces never fit the same as before. Max had colic, wanted only me. So I held him twenty-four hours a day, tied to my body in his baby bundler, and vacuumed the living room for hours because it was the only thing other than nursing that soothed him. If anyone else, including his father, grandparents, early childhood teachers, neighbors, grocery clerks, even Sophie, so much as looked at Max, he might cry.

And I blamed myself for his colic, because of that scary woman at the therapy group, the moaner who threatened to bring a gun and shoot us all in that awful fluorescent basement. *Bang, bang, bang,* she said, cocking her finger. I brought my unborn son with me into that den of despair and wrath and goneness, I carried him there inside my spoiled body, week after week, to endure what was beyond anyone's ability to endure. I did *that* to my perfect boy, and now I could never, ever take it back.

That first year, Max cried and nursed until my nipples bled and scabbed and bled again. I contracted a raging case of mastitis. A storm raged in me, spiraled right through fall into winter. Snow fell, snow melted. When new growth poked through the mud, so, too, did memories. Groves and thickets of the past, pushing into the present. Spring warmed to summer and summer fell to autumn. Winter, in its cruelty, came again. Now it was not just Mafia and my childhood self who intruded, but also fresh knowledge of the woman I had allowed myself to become. During those long winter days snowed in with two small children, I slowly recalled things from my recent past. Incredulous things. Like that stretchy black bodysuit I wore for John on our first wedding anniversary at the Hotel Luxe, when Sophie was not quite six weeks old, my lumpy post-partum body stuffed into that tube of Lycra with its sexy crotch hole for my still raw episiotomy scar from the jagged knife wound where the anonymous male doctor had sliced all the way through the tough muscle of my vaginal wall and every other layer of muscle to follow until the blade came out the other side, leaving not only a gash but a swollen bruise *the size of a grapefruit.* That's what John had said the day we got home from the hospital with our firstborn, what he said when I asked him to look down there because it hurt so much I couldn't breathe, what he said before he turned white and slid down the wall: *the size of a grapefruit.*

Time and again that second winter with Max, when he was one year old and still fragile— "highly sensitive," the books said—it all came flooding back, that body suit and firm mattress, my young husband desperate to *come like a freight train, six weeks is a long time, are you okay*, me floating out and away. I became so electric that winter that if Sophie so much as nipped me, one little bite that barely hurt, just an attempt, really, not even a real bite, I would throw her favorite book across the room and smash its binding. That March, Baby Girl brought in fleas, fleas that chose me as their human host, red bites up and down my ankles and calves, diatomaceous earth—chemicals will kill you—coating our wood floors, clinging to the soles of our feet, sticking to our clothes, grinding into our sheets. Finally, the sunny morning when Sophie eyed her baby brother in his adorable striped rugby suit, pink and blue—he was eighteen months and walking now, in that teetering and tentative way that toddlers walk, so fragile you can blow them down with one strong puff. Sophie watched him quietly and long as he toddled his way through a shaft of light on the oak floor. Then she shoved him hard into the corner of the banister. The edges of the room darkened around me, closed into a shadowy tunnel, through which I lunged to slap my firstborn daughter across the cheek. I watched my handprint bloom like a hibiscus.

I wanted to die.

What happened next was swift and irrevocable—its own kind of doorway. "You know, I lied," I told John in the middle of another fight about sex, and how angry he was over not getting it. Angry that I "had two legs and should know how to use them." Angry that I was, as he now said, frigid. "I lied and lied," I said again, as Max nursed greedily with his whole body. "I never had nine orgasms with you back in the beginning. I never even had one. And I still haven't."

I thought of my therapist, what she said about women and sex. "You could at least try," I said meanly. "Slow down and use your hands." But that's not all. God, he was a hard worker, my young husband. A two-hour round-trip commute to an inner-city middle school by day, two shifts a week at the night school, too, walking through the door after ten o'clock for what? Laundry. Although with Max, at least, we had a diaper service. I had demanded that, now that I demanded things. Still, diapers were nothing in a sea of everything, and whatever else needed doing, John did it. He did. But that didn't stop me from telling him how I'd been pretending. It didn't stop me from pushing him away from me with all the force I could muster.

———

The day after the biscuits and gravy, we drive with Sophie and Max all the way to Minneapolis and even farther, to Fort Snelling, where the Mississippi and Minnesota rivers converge. Wind pummels us back and forth in our lane, whines eerily through the windows of our big blue sedan. The kids are in high spirits. Sophie, especially, is all soprano chatter. She leans over onto Max's car seat, whispers brightly that her spirit animal used to be a squirrel, but isn't anymore. "Now it's a sugar glider, Max," she says. "Baby sugar gliders live in their mamas' pouches like kangaroos. They look like flying squirrels. But they're not." Max listens, wide-eyed, as his sister explains the many differences between rodents and marsupials.

John's eyes are glued to the road, chin set. I think of putting my hand on his thigh. Sophie is telling Max about how the boy sugar gliders don't have pouches, they have furry "scroters." I miss Sophie's horse phase for its sheer comedy, but I am besotted with her at four. Her banter is delicious.

At Fort Snelling, we wander around the historic walled fort with its nineteenth-century stone buildings and monuments, browning grass fields. The kids can run in any direction with nothing to stop them: no roads or obstacles, no parents yelling *stop* or *no*. There is nowhere for them to disappear and nothing we need to regulate, really, yet John and I stand at attention at the edge of the field, tracking them out of habit. Max is chasing Sophie with all he's got.

"He's so determined," John says.

"Someday he'll outpace her," I say. I reach for John's hand. "I love you." I squeeze his thick fingers, press my arm into his, warm and solid through his nylon jacket. My husband. I rest my cheek on his chest and feel his heartbeat in my own ear, even through layers of clothing. We could call this desire. I kiss him. He lets me. I open my mouth against his, explore his lips and tongue as if for the first time.

Twenty feet away, Sophie and Max are screaming, "Steer toward the island! The engine's still going!" Amelia Earhart is their latest disaster game. These tragic re-enactments were, in fact, the beginning of the end of Sophie's horse antics. Amelia Earhart is her favorite, surely, but Amelia's mysterious disappearance is only one of the many tragedies that Sophie and Max love. Others include the wreck of the Edmund Fitzgerald, the sinking of the Titanic, the Hindenburg explosion, various nonspecific incidents in the Bermuda Triangle and the Sargasso Sea, and a handful of obscure nautical mishaps they know by heart from their *Shipwrecks of the Great Lakes* cassette tape.

Now, in this windy field, flying their imaginary Electra brings out the wild in these children, reddens their cheeks and sweeps back their hair. Their unzipped nylon jackets billow behind them like flags. John wraps his arm around me as we watch. "You're the co-pilot," Sophie yells. "I'm *Amelia!*" She's always Amelia. For the next hour, our children fly their plane, crash land it, and start over—a continuous loop. There is nothing else to do. After the crash landing, they have no script. No one does.

When the already gray light eventually shifts and the temperature drops by several degrees, the children grow cold and cross and their play devolves into bickering. We pile back into the car and the end of wind comes as a terrific relief to all of us. We become quiet and relax into the dry heat and gentle rocking of Big Blue—that is what we call this giant old Plymouth, inherited from John's parents for the price of an expensive transmission repair. The children eat peanut butter sandwiches and drink from thermoses of hot chocolate. When their chatter stops and they drift to sleep, the backseat fills with their steady breathing, their chorus of air. At home, we carry their sleeping bodies, heavy as donkeys, into the house to their beds. So deeply asleep are they that we leave them in their clothes, smelling of cold wind and sweat, only pulling off, with care, their shoes and jackets. We crawl into bed ourselves, and I pull John on top of me and inside of me until he comes, quickly and urgently.

Her name will be Lillian. It means, *I vow.*

More

John and I are in the kitchen, filling plastic containers with Thanksgiving leftovers while the kids watch *Beauty and the Beast*. Sophie strongly prefers the Beast to Gaston. *Strongly* prefers. I'm about to laugh about this, share the comedy with John, when it washes over me, a sudden recognition. "Déjà vu," I say.

"About what?" he says.

"Everything. Everything that's happening right now—like walking into this precise moment, except it also stretches open into past and future, like an accordion, to include our leaving Center City, moving back to Minneapolis. It feels like a dream, where I'm walking through the kitchen or cleaning the tub or whatever, and I'm feeling like, 'oh my god, what have we done, moving here.' Which is stupid, because every day I wake up so happy to be here. So happy we moved. It makes no sense."

"Weird," John says. I don't tell him that this feeling sometimes lasts all day. That I prowl the house touching things to remind myself of what I love: the picture window, the wild roses out front, the tree swing out back, the unfinished attic where I hope one day to make a bedroom under the tall branches. All this noticing and appreciating mostly works, for a while, at least, to chase away the weird false memory of mistake.

I'm covering the pies—pumpkin and pecan—in plastic wrap. Earlier, I burned my left hand on the oven rack. It still throbs. I blink back tears when my wedding ring catches itself on the drawer pull. This ring, a tenth-anniversary gift from John. A one-carat diamond in a simple platinum setting. I finally asked for something to replace the ring John had remade from the original engagement ring he'd chosen for his first fiancée, the girl who came before me and had my same name, spelled differently. I am not used to the Tiffany-style setting, the way it stands at attention. Always, I am getting my hand caught up on things.

"Are you okay?" John says.

"Just tired." I lean deep into the refrigerator to make room for the cranberries. "And lonely."

"Why lonely?" John sounds as if he's actually curious. As if he genuinely wants to hear more about my loneliness.

"Because of us," I say. "How distant we are. It scares me, and I don't know how to fix it."

"We're fine, Jeannie," he says. "The kids are fine. Money is fine, for once. Look, everything's fine. Let's enjoy it."

"I feel like we're in separate boats," I say. "Separate boats on a big lake. It's cold and windy and the rain is sheeting down and I'm trying to row over to you—I can see you over there in your boat—but no matter how hard I row, I don't get closer. And if—"

"If boat is some kind of metaphor for sex, don't worry. I'm fine," John says. He's been seeing a sex therapist this past year, by my request. I started feeling some real desire again around the time of Lillie's second birthday, when she started nursing so much less. Now, at four, she nurses only occasionally for comfort. I have plenty of desire. It just never gets fulfilled. In fact, the more I want, the worse it gets. *Faster, faster, faster.*

"What do you mean, you're fine?" I say.

"I mean, I'm fine now, and I was fine before all this business with the shrinky dink. Besides, as long as you won't do the exercises, what's the point?"

At first, I did do those sex therapy exercises with John—stop, pinch, pull, breathe, start over, and so on—but I simply could not stand it. Turning our already strained sexual encounters into such detached exchanges was traumatic in a way I couldn't fully explain but couldn't overcome, either. It made me feel four years old again, asexual but sexualized. Completely exposed. So, John was left to practice on his own. If he chose to.

"I tried those exercises," I say. "But it's not really something I can fix, is it?"

"Maybe nothing needs fixing," he says. "Like I said, I was fine before you started all this."

"You were fine whether or not it felt good to me?"

John turns now from the pan he is scraping over the sink. Sets the pan on the counter and looks at me, hard and slow. "Don't take this wrong, okay?" he says. "But, maybe you just can't, you know? Maybe you're frigid, and nothing will ever feel good to you."

"That's the meanest thing you've ever said," I say, even though he has said it many times before. The frigid part, that is. This time, though, it's different. Colder. He's not angry, and it's not an accusation. It's a diagnosis. He's given this some thought, and arrived at a conclusion.

"I said don't take it wrong," he says. "I'm just wondering, is all. I tried your woo-woo tantra stuff. I tried your sex therapy. What else do you want?"

"We could try tantra again," I say. "Take it more seriously. We could try holding hands, even. Cuddling, for fuck's sake. This isn't just about sex, John. It's about being *close*. Being in love again. Remember when we thought we were soulmates? We're going to end up like your parents."

"My parents have been married for forty years."

"I know, but are they in love?"

"Seriously?" he says. "You're asking if my parents love each other?"

"No. I'm asking if they're *in love*."

"Jeannie, they've been successfully married for almost half a century. Life isn't a movie. At least I learned that much from my parents." He pauses. "What did you learn from your parents?"

This is a thing John does when we fight—lobs attacks at my parents. As if I can help how they lived their lives, how they're still living their lives. But that's not what he's talking about now. I understand this. He's saying our problems stem from my parents' problems, manifested in me. And it's true, I suppose. My parents did teach me things.

First and foremost, maybe forever, they taught me to want more.

Big Blue

The thing I miss most about living in the country is the very thing I eventually came to hate about it: the long snake of black tar between one place and another, the empty distances, the endless driving. Oh my God, how I miss the driving.

I miss the reasons for the all that driving, too. The days and days without leaving the house in winter, little babies, creaky floors, nowhere to go, no one to see. Four walls, big window, bare branches, frozen lake, empty sidewalks. Everything blank. I miss the desperate escape of stuffing the babies into snowsuits and then stuffing those snowsuits into car seats, clicking them in, and going, going, nowhere, sometimes for hours. Sleeping children, warm car, barren county roads. I can't remember anymore the times it didn't work. The times the baby boy screamed instead of slept, the times the spirited girl, that untamed horse, grew cross and pulled his hair or bit him.

The car I most hated driving is the one I now recall so fondly. Big Blue. She was not only large but unstylish, with a dangling patch of duct tape on the taillight (to note, that taillight had been smashed while Big Blue sat innocently in the small-town church parking lot during the Mass that John's parents were attending). But I don't remember the duct tape anymore, or how people looked at me when I drove that car, with expressions that made me feel like a cross between a grandpa and a teen mom. No, that's not at all the way I remember Big Blue now. It's the heft I recall, the solid slam of the door, the soft, steady way the car hummed at high speeds— never any shaking or whining like the small tin box I drive today. Big Blue had a way of rocking gently on the highway that made me understand and appreciate the likening of large cars to watercraft.

It's a compliment, really, to call a car a boat. I loved Big Blue, even though I was very, very happy when she died.

What I miss most about those country afternoons in Big Blue is the way it came to feel so normal to drive a long way to nowhere. Sometimes I took the children to the thrift store at the intersection that still poses as a town called Almelund. I'd carry Max on my hip while chasing Sophie through the aisles. But the chase was made easier by the woman who owned the shop—her strange appearance entranced my curious little girl. The shopkeeper always wore floor-length skirts with aprons, and frilly blouses with high collars, small buttons, and puffed sleeves. She looked like Ma Ingalls on Sunday. I don't know why the shopkeeper dressed this way, because I never asked her. But she fit in well with her surroundings. The air in the shop was dense with must, and the place was crammed floor to ceiling with broken antiques and unusual junk. I always, out of politeness, bought some tiny thing, usually a ten-cent plastic toy to keep my eager filly occupied for the long drive home.

Just as often as we stopped, we would also keep going, further east into Wisconsin or north toward Pine City, children sleeping, motor whirring, road unrolling behind us like the world's longest runner, steel gray and utterly inhospitable except for its openness. The only choices to be made were trivial. Turn left or right? Exit now or later? Turn around or keep on driving?

I miss driving like that because I'll never do it again. The country is behind me, with its right-wing politics and greasy-spoon food and frigid lake full of milfoil and disappointment. The country with its endless county roads crisscrossing each other and looping back on themselves, as senseless and difficult to decipher as the lines of an open palm. So many roads, so few destinations.

My children don't wear snowsuits anymore, or ride in car seats, or remember much about Big Blue. They are grown and have places to go with specific routes to appointed stops that leave little room for rumination. Like all cities, Minneapolis is full of destinations. A city crammed with beauty and filth, fields like amber oceans and blighted summer parking lots soft as dough, clover and creeping thistle under chain link, winter snow melting into gutters, and most of all, people, people with their mouths full of food and gum and each other's tongues, acid-washed jeans and men's wool overcoats from the surplus store reeking of mothballs and old sweat, hair stiff with gel, red Solo cups and warm skin. A city is electric and overflowing. But it is short on long stretches of tar, time, and space, the kind of stretches where a person can travel hundreds of miles without ever leaving. I never, ever want to drive that way again, so desperately and without destination, but, still, I miss it more than I can say.

Trace a Path

When I tell the story of the last time I got kicked out of the family—the last time before foster care that is—and how I finally went looking for Eve, I often forget to start at the beginning, which is to say that the day I leave for Mexico, April 9, 1984, is my sixteenth birthday. *My home is your home. You're like another daughter to me. Don't forget that.*

Rachael does not want me to go—she is ten now—but she promises not to tell Mom. I promise her something, too. "We will come back for you," I say. "Eve will help, after I tell her everything."

My hands tremble a little at the bus station as I fish crumpled twenty-dollar bills from the inside pocket of my purple *Ciao!* tote bag. I have been working after school at Arby's for almost a year now. Three dollars and thirty-five cents an hour doesn't add up fast, but I do have enough cash for this sixty-seven-dollar one-way bus ticket to El Paso, plus forty dollars extra. I'm worried, though. Can this woman behind the glass, with her clicking-clacking red fingernails, call the police? Report me as a suspected runaway? My heart is a trapped animal bashing itself against my sternum. But the woman doesn't even look up. She just hands me my ticket and warns me not to lose it. "I mean it," she says. "They won't let you back on the bus if you do."

In just over an hour, I am settled into my cushiony bus seat and the Greyhound terminal is growing smaller and smaller behind me. From the city of El Paso, I will be able to walk across an international bridge to Juarez. That's what the encyclopedia says. After I cross the bridge, I'm not sure. I think there are trains. At least my Spanish is pretty good. I'm the best student in my tenth-grade class.

Of the bus ride, I remember little: the whir of the tires below, the murmur of other voices rising and falling, the dirty bathroom and the way I try not to drink too much water in order to avoid it. The middle-of-the-night rest stop in Oklahoma City. "Fifteen minutes!" the driver says as we passengers, loose-limbed with sleep, feel our way through aisle, out the door, and down the steps to find bathrooms and snacks at the Stop-and-Shop, to use payphones and smoke cigarettes. Six minutes later, I am back in my seat. Other people take their time. The lady behind me takes a little too much. Shouts erupt from the back of the bus—*Wait! Someone's coming! What the fuck, man!*—but we're already turning out of the lot, onto the on ramp, the lady running alongside, then behind, waving her arms, hollering words we cannot hear.

Another day and night later, we disembark mid-morning in El Paso. I am getting nervous about this supposed bridge—how to find it, how to walk across it, what will happen on the other side. That's why I wander without direction until I find a gas station, where I browse for food—string cheese, Ritz crackers, Tab, and, for later, a king size bag of sunflower seeds and a pack of Starburst. They don't have Jolly Ranchers here. I lean against the brick exterior of the store to eat and wait my turn for the bathroom. The key dangles from an oversized plastic ruler, which is sticky. So is the bathroom—but it's better than the one on the bus. I rummage in my bag for deodorant, a toothbrush, my powder compact to soak up the oil on my face. I wet the corner of a brown paper towel and rub at the half-moons of mascara under my eyes. Then I put on more.

Downtown El Paso is big. Bigger than Minneapolis, I think. But if I just keep going around this block, then the next, and back again, in and out in concentric squares, I will not get lost. Anyway, after three days on the bus, it feels good to walk, my mouth full of salty sunflower seeds to spit on the sidewalk when no one is looking. It is late afternoon by the time I stop at the park, the one with a giant stone sculpture of an Aztec calendar. I have walked by it several times already, but now two boys with black jeans and side-swept hair are leaning against the base of the calendar. One has a Walkman, and the melody of "Walking on Sunshine" floats out, tinny and thin. They boys raise up their beer cans. "Hey, foxy," they say. "Wanna party?" The boy with the longer hair holds out his beer can, and I raise it to my lips, sip a little. I do not like beer. These boys don't seem to think it's that weird that I came all the way from Minnesota, just got off the Greyhound. They want to know if I've met Paul Bunyan. "Like, you guys have real lumberjacks and shit?" The bridge, they say, is nearby. "Straight that way," they say in unison, pointing, laughing. "But don't go yet," the one with the longer hair says. "First, another sixer." We walk across the park to the Shell Station.

By the time I am standing on the bridge, I have pretended to drink enough beer that I feel it, that strange tingle behind my forehead. The sun hangs low already, silhouetting buildings and blurring the shapes of those boys as I walk away. The bridge itself both does and does not look like the black and white photo in the encyclopedia. On the one hand, a bridge is a bridge. But I have never walked across such a big one. Long lines of cars crawl in both directions, windows down, barely moving. Everything else, though, seems to sway, like the giant flags rippling over the throng of pedestrians pushing strollers, swinging mesh shopping bags, and balancing everything at once—boom boxes on their shoulders, children on their hips, the distance between themselves and others.

Juarez is more crowded than El Paso—noisier, busier, hotter, denser with bodies and food smells, stray animals and litter, heavy traffic and exhaust, honking horns, squealing breaks. Street vendors yell, too, in loud, fast Spanish I do not understand. Here, I am not so certain about walking in concentric squares. Here, the streets—or avenidas—lack the same block formations I am used to. Instead they cut at diagonals, lead to dead ends and round-a-bouts, curve mid-block in ways I don't expect. People might be staring at me. Men, especially. I try not to stare back. They whistle and whoop and say gringa—a word I know.

At first, there are women, too, on the sidewalks, old women arm in arm, young women with gleaming hair swaying behind them, mothers tugging at their children's arms. But the longer I walk, the fewer women I see. Dusk falls quickly in April. I am no longer certain where the bridge is. Ahead of me, a man with a brown beer bottle, swerving. Across the street, two men strolling side by side, roaring with laughter, one with his arm draped around the shoulder of the other. Behind me, a man alone, whistling. Sitting against a pink brick building, an old man with sunken eyes and no teeth, a wooden bowl in his hand. Exiting a tiny grocery store to my left, a man in a jean jacket, short hair, steady pace.

"Perdóneme," I say. The man keeps walking. "Perdóneme!" I say again, louder. He turns, quizzical, says something in Spanish. The two men across the street yell things I don't like, even if I don't know what they are. "Donde esta el estación?" I say to the man from the grocery store, enunciating every word. I don't remember the word for train. "La estación de autobus?" I am not sure which is correct here, train or bus, el or la. The man babbles softly in Spanish, nods, turns up his palms. "Donde esta la estación?" I say again and again. The men across the street whistle like crazy now, say something about chica, something about sexy. "Por favor?" I say to the man from the grocery store. What is the word for help? "Ayuda?" I say, unsure. "Por favor?" I say. "Por *favor*?" Finally, he seems to understand, motions me to follow as he hurries toward the intersection, turns left, cuts across the street, then continues several blocks as the last rays of sunlight warm our backs. We come to a plain, three-story building, tan stucco. I have never seen a train station, but this does not appear to be one.

"Estación?" I say. What is the word? "*Train?*" I say.

"No, no, sígueme." He opens the door and waits for me to step through it, but my legs don't move. I have been traveling alone for four days. I have twenty-four dollars left. For the first time since leaving St. Paul, I am afraid.

"Estación?"

"Sigueme, por favor?" he says, still holding the door.

The sun has slid fully beneath the skyline. At the end of the block, four adult men cluster outside a storefront. *Guera bonita!* The man from the grocery store puts his hand on my shoulder now, steers me into the building. At sixteen years and four days old, 1,381 miles from home, I wait patiently behind this stranger as he speaks in muffled Spanish to a woman behind a barred window. She hands him something. He waves me toward a narrow staircase. This is not a train station. At the top of the stairs, the man uses what I now see is a key to open the door to what looks like a hotel room. Maybe I am wrong, though. Maybe he lives here, and needs to do something or get something before taking me to the station. He pats the top of the bed—its shiny pink bedspread—and says more things in Spanish before stepping into the bathroom. *Solo un minuto* are the last words I hear, the only words I understand. My teacher would be so disappointed.

————

Outside the window, blackness. Inside, the sound of running water, a warm fog. So soothing, this humid indoor air, after the biting wind of the bridge, the evening cool of the street. I sense the rocking of the bus, the whir of its tires—then I jerk myself awake again, pull myself back up into the room, tell myself I cannot fall asleep. But here I go, losing my hold again, and again, until I slip, finally, into nothingness. Maybe I sleep for minutes. Maybe an hour. The room is darker, and my head is thick with something like fever. A faucet squeaking and something else, a swish. Clinking and tapping. The bathroom door releases a cloud of steam and aftershave, and the man, wearing a white towel around his waist, moving toward the bed, leaning over me, his face so close I can see the open pores in his skin and the sheen on his eyelashes.

I lurch back against the plaster wall, pull my arms around my legs. "I need the train station," I say. "La estación. Autobus. Anything. Please." It comes to me, the word for train: "Entrenar," I say. I will not cry. "Por favor," I say. "I am Catholic." I'm speaking entirely in English now. "A Catholic girl," I say. "*Catholic*. I love Jesus and God and . . . " I fold my hands in prayer, close my eyes. "I love the Virgin Mary. I love the Virgin. Please. Help me."

"Estaba equivocado," he says, backing away, crossing himself. "Lo siento, lo siento." He's at the wooden chair by the window now, gathering his clothes, moving toward the bathroom. "Entendí mal," he says. My tote bag is still on the bed with me. I check the inside pocket—my money is there. I pull my canvas tennis shoes on without tying them, but the chain lock on the door is sticky. "No, no vayas!" the man says. He is dressed now, digging through his wallet. He holds out what looks like a driver's license. "Lo siento. Mi corazón!" He holds out the license for me to take. I hold it under the dim glow of the wall sconce, but it means nothing to me. Now, he sweeps his arms toward the bed, but sits himself on that hard-backed chair. "Te prometo," he says, crossing himself again. "Te prometo, te prometo." Maybe I believe him. Maybe I have no choice. Either way, I half sleep—still in my jeans and sweater, my windbreaker and my untied shoes—on top of that shiny pink bedspread, while the man sits upright in that wooden chair, his head against the wall.

Night lasts forever. In the morning, the man speaks of the estacion, the entrenar. He takes us to a street-side café where we eat chilaquiles and drink sweet horchata before walking to the train station, where he speaks to the border agent in long melodic sentences. I catch something about identification, because he repeats it so many times. But I have none. I haven't even gotten my permit yet—driver's ed is expensive, and, anyway, I only just turned sixteen. The border agent is about to turn away, until the man from the grocery store bends down and whispers something in his ear. They both laugh, turn red in the face. The agent claps the man on the back, and suddenly I am boarding the train, finding my place among the women and children and babies—a few men, too, lots of chickens, two goats—as the train pulls away toward Chihuahua City, where I will board an express bus to Mexico City before transferring, finally, to one bound for Cuernavaca.

Four nights after leaving home and more than two thousand miles later, I step into the Cuernavaca terminal. The lobby is small and almost cheerful, a curved service counter with smiling attendants in red uniforms and jaunty hats. I am tired and hungry. My clothes are filthy. I haven't seen myself in a mirror since El Paso. But I made it. I can't wait to tell Eve I am here. She will be so surprised. But, there are some things I don't know. Like how to find Eve's phone number. "Libra telefono?" I say to the woman at the ticket counter.

"Que?"

I hold a pretend phone to my ear and open my palms like a book. The woman says something I don't understand. Everyone speaks too fast. I swipe some tears and try again, in my worthless Spanish. The woman steps out from behind the counter, puts her arm around me. "No estés triste," she says. Triste, I know, means sad. She takes me into to an office, patting my back as we go. She wants me to sit in a chair while she calls the English-speaking radio station—apparently this is the best way to communicate with Cuernavaca's large American expat community. Soon, a young woman from the radio station picks me up in her green Volkswagen. She zips us down a maze of narrow, bumpy streets. "Don't worry too much," she says, adjusting the strap of her tank top and checking her rearview mirror. "Everyone here knows someone who knows someone. We'll find your friend."

At her apartment—just one large room with a bed, table, couch, tiny stove and refrigerator—she makes more phone calls in Spanish. Her radio is on, and the DJ at the English-speaking radio station asks about Eve on air every few minutes, encouraging people to call in if they have information.

By late afternoon, someone at the American library has arranged with an American pastor and his wife to let me stay in the parsonage overnight. But now the questions won't stop coming.

How can we contact your parents?

I'm sorry, we can't. They are vacationing in Europe for a month, and unreachable. That's why they sent me to stay with Eve, our family friend.

But if arrangements were made in advance . . ?

I guess Eve got the dates of my visit wrong?

Are there any relatives or friends to call?

Not really. My grandparents are dead, and both of my parents are only children. They don't have—it's just, we move a lot for my dad's job. He's a businessman.

Your luggage . . . is this tote bag all you brought for the month?

No, no. It's just, I forgot my suitcase in Kansas City—the bus leaves so quickly. They'll leave you behind if you're late.

I am beginning to understand, with certainty, that Eve is no longer in Cuernavaca. She must have moved again. It seems everyone else is beginning to understand this, too.

"Muy extraño," the young woman says to the pastor. She has driven me here, helped me to explain the situation in English. But now they have switched to Spanish for this side conversation, Spanish I suddenly understand perfectly well in every way: their reasons for speaking it, the words themselves, and the way they are looking at each other. Still, I am very happy I will be staying here in the parsonage guestroom, with its open-air terrace jutting out over the cobblestone streets of this steep hillside, crumbling stone walls bursting with bright bougainvillea and Jacaranda trees swaying in the wind. I never knew air could smell like this. But I do know what will happen next. How the pastor will eventually reach my mom, who will call my dad, who will buy my plane ticket home. I guess he will have no choice.

A Chronology of New Years

New Year's Eve, 1978, Wyoming

I am ten and hunched alone in my bedroom, listening to my new transistor radio—brown leatherette, a Christmas gift mailed to me by my father. I'm not truly alone in my room, though, because I share it with my baby sister. She's three, and sleeps noisily in her bed, face to the wall. I want the number-one song on the countdown to be "Grease." My Christmas candy is long gone, but I do still have my sugar egg diorama from last Easter. The sugar egg is not for eating, though—it is a knick-knack. It sits on my dresser next to my jewelry box. Still, I lick it. It tastes like dust and school glue, but sweeter. I take the first bite. The number one song is not "Grease." It is "Shadow Dancing."

New Year's Eve, 1985, Lake Phalen

"Careless Whisper" tops the charts, but I like the number-two song, "Like a Virgin." I'm seventeen and watching for my boyfriend. The window is thickly frosted on the inside, and I scrape a heart into the ice with my fingernail. This room I share with the other foster girls overlooks Lake Phalen, which itself is a mean sheet of ice crusted over with spurs of light. My boyfriend is late. He doesn't love me but I love him. He has a car—a vintage Cadillac hearse. I can see the hearse coming from far away. He'll pull into the driveway, even though the foster parents don't like it when he does that. The downstairs is their real house, where they live with their real kids. Only the upstairs is a group home. A buzzer rings every time we foster kids open our door at the bottom of the back stairs. But after the midnight curfew, that door is locked. If the buzzer rings then, the police are called. I have only been late once.

New Year's Eve, 1988, Deer Lake

I met my new boyfriend, John, at a college telemarketing job. He is a few years older than I am and he drives a perfectly normal car. I don't have my license yet. John teaches middle school social studies. We are celebrating New Year's Eve with his two good friends and their wives at his parents' house, which sits sturdily on its slope above Deer Lake. His parents are out for the evening. With John's friends, we plan to cook seafood and drink wine. "Trust me, this will taste just like lobster," one of the men says, unwrapping a fishy package. The women talk about their jobs in marketing and human resources. They talk about the cost of fabric for drapes in their three-bedroom homes. They talk about having babies. I am twenty years old. My younger sister, at fourteen, is still in foster care. At my apartment, I often make boxed macaroni and cheese and eat it from the pot while watching TV. This year's biggest hit is "Faith." Next year, I will marry this man.

New Year's Eve, 1990, The Dinner Bell

Sophie is five months old. Her top lip has one perfect white blister from nursing, which she does ecstatically and with her whole self. When she is sated, she goes limp—"drunken sailor," her father says, and milk pools, sticky, in the spaces where her skin meets mine. Tonight, my husband's parents are babysitting. We are young, they said. Young people must go out on New Year's Eve. My dress pinches around my swollen breasts. In the grim light of the Dinner Bell bathroom, I see someone else's face. "Not bad," my husband says about the gluey mass of noodles on his plate. He is trying. We both are. Sophie lies in her crib in our house, a drafty Victorian fixer-upper with beautiful bones perched high on the crest of Summit Avenue. The house looks out over the blackness of North Center Lake. Sophie is a seabird. She flies into the world through me. My glass case breaks and breaks and breaks. Fresh air rushes in, merciless. The number one song this year is "Hold On."

New Year's Eve, 2000 – 2014, Home

By the time of the divorce, I have three beautiful children. So does the man I have fallen hard into love with, the man who becomes my second husband. Together, we try to stitch a family together from scraps and remnants. We create new holiday traditions, including epic New Year's celebrations with our closest friends, for which we make cheese fondue and chocolate-dipped rose petals and home-made bread. Our six kids and their friends pile into our house for endless games of Monopoly and Risk. We even let them build a mini golf course with sand traps in an upstairs bedroom. They spill punch and trail crumbs all over the house while we adults toast our next opportunity for a clean slate. Some years, we read fortunes or write our regrets on slips of paper for burning. The kids run around the block banging pots and pans. One year, we make martinis and get drunk enough to gyrate ecstatically to "Dancing Queen" while saying and doing impossibly embarrassing things. Mostly, though, we are lucid for these turning points. We look back, we look forward. Why, then, as the years pass, do we not see it coming? Hear it coming? This feathery ruckus, the frantic then steady beating of wings, as these kids slice into the air, one after the next? The New Year's Eve before our youngest takes flight, the top song is "Happy." You should hear how it is now, this clanging of radiators against the rise and fall of our bodies and our breath, my husband's and mine, echoing inside the ribs of this empty house.

New Year's Eve, Forward, The Body

The year turns on the calendar, yes, but also in our bodies. Not long into 2015, I wake to a text from our youngest: *Mama! I will take care of you when you are old!* I am only forty-six then, but her message is inspired by loss and example. My husband's 95-year-old mother had recently died, and we were all so moved by how tenderly his sister cared for her. Perhaps the turning of the year is always as much a burial as a birth, a marked page more than a blank one. English novelist Graham Greene wrote of the winter holidays, "[W]e require a season when we can regret all the flaws in our human relationships: it is the feast of failure, sad but consoling." Still, next time one year gives way to the next, I'll put my feet on the floor and look forward and say, *I'm alive!* If I were the resolution-making type, I'd resolve to love harder. I'd wish that for all of us: to love more ferociously, this bruised up planet and each other, to love with our muscles and our bones and our spectacular teeth, our eyelashes and our precise, unmistakable skin—inscribed as it is with the scars and abrasions of where we've been. We can love loudly with our voices, too, singing and humming and hissing into the ether from within these strange and temporary shells that hold us.

Bent

Daughterhood Recalled Through Skin and Bone

with Lillian Ouellette-Howitz

I.

Mama tells me stories. Some, I make her tell me again and again. Like the one where she was three years old and rolled her neighbor's pool balls, slick and shiny, down the buckled sidewalk of 24th Street. I like to imagine those balls, wild and free, careening down the steep hill to the rocky shores of Lake Superior below. Some of Mama's stories are so real they grow inside me, like a baby.

Fetuses can hear sounds in utero at eighteen weeks. The noise is bent, distorted through liquid, skin, and bone. Still, research shows that a baby will remember and prefer her mother's voice over all others. One study recorded mothers speaking, then linked those recordings to sensors in baby bottles. When a baby sucked hard enough, she heard her mother, but when she sucked more softly, she heard a stranger. All of the babies sucked hard enough to hear their mothers. A mother's voice, researchers say, is like a neural fingerprint in her child's brain. We are still learning how much is passed down through genes. Can memories be inherited, like dimples? I don't know. But I know my story, and Mama's.

Remember the story of my headache? I mean, your headache? I'm pretty sure I was the one driving, but it could have been your dad.

My story is not my Mama's story.

Because your dad and I were still—and you were a tiny thing. Barely two.

I was in my body.

Either way, Auntie was riding next to you in the back of the Volvo. You were in your car seat, sobbing. "What's the matter?" Auntie said, eyes stretched wide. She put her hand on your doughy little thigh, bare-skinned and sweaty.

I could feel all the parts of myself.

"Mama has a headache," you cried, clutching your own head between your hands. "And it's hurting me. Hurting me!"

II.

When Mama was pregnant, she read books. So many books about babies and children and motherhood. She loved Alice Miller, D.W. Winnicott, Penelope Leach, John Bowlby. She called her books her bibles. I, on the other hand, call them textbooks. My degree is in early childhood development. I have studied the intricacies of conception through birth and beyond. Still, I hold onto my childhood image of Mama's womb as a cozy room inside her with shelves of toys and books and a bed where someone tucks me in at night.

I was afraid to grow a child in my body because of Mafia. What he did to me all those years. The oiliness of him, his calluses and fingernails. Trauma, they say, is coded into our genes, mapped into our DNA. Trauma, they say, shapes us and our children for generations to come. Still, I had you. Still, I have you.

Over time, Mama's stories wove themselves together into a singular truth of the human my Mama was before me. I don't remember how old I was when I first heard each story, but I am pretty sure about the order of events. First came the wilted roses, then the bus driver, then the abortion. And, of course, Mafia. Grandma's second husband. But I think I always knew about him—at least a little.

The idea is, trauma leaves a chemical mark on a person's genes. That's how *The New York Times* explained it. The article said the mark doesn't directly damage the gene. Instead, it alters the mechanism by which the gene is *expressed*: "The alteration isn't genetic. It's epigenetic."

III.

The first time I heard the Milo story, I must have been in middle school, because the kitchen walls were still bright yellow. I was perched on a stool at the counter. The morning had left warm light pooling across the cupboards and floors. Mama was seventeen when she met Milo. She was riding the bus to her foster home, the one where they locked the kids in at night, because it was easier that way. Milo drove the bus. He was old, in his thirties, at least, and had an ex-wife and kids. Mama's foster sister—her name was Joy—started it, the idea of Milo, of riding his bus home late. The first time Milo kissed Mama was at the end of his route, in one of those parking garages where all of the buses pull off for the night. It was nearly spring, and the snow was half-melted, leftover and forgotten. But the ground was still frozen and hard under its dirty blanket. I studied Mama's face as she spoke to me in the kitchen that day. I created images in my mind of this man, with his early balding and too-big jeans. He was so sad. I could feel his sad in my chest. Resting on top of my lungs. And Mama. This was the moment it struck me, the completeness of her humanity. I held her face in my hands. "That was you," I told her. "This body. This skin. These bones. You were there."

But the kitchen walls were yellow until we moved from that house—which was after you started college. Remember? So, I think you were older for the Milo story. Anyway, epigenetics is the science of what we carry in our skin and bones, what sleeps in our genes and travels through generations, ultimately waking up or not in response to our life experiences. On the one hand, we can't control heredity. We get what we get. On the other hand, not everything underground will quicken come spring. When I was a kid, my mother smoked and got divorced. I swore I'd never do either.

During the autumn of the divorce, Mama hid cigarettes in the basement. I was in kindergarten then. I remember having what my teachers called an "off day." I was spacey, sensitive, quieter than usual. In the carpool line after school, I stood watching as one car after the next came with open windows and smiling blonde mothers. I watched little backpacks disappear and snacks get pulled out of crisp white paper bags. I counted the cars until my dad's Volvo rounded the bend. Then, as my brother and sister folded themselves into the backseat, I turned and ran as fast as I could.

There are times, still, when I want to run. Wasn't it Goethe who said, "If I knew myself, I'd run away?" The same *New York Times* article that explained epigenetics disputed the theory: "Headlines suggest that the epigenetic marks of trauma can be passed from one generation to the next. But the evidence, at least in humans, is circumstantial at best."

IV.

I was in my body until I wasn't. Then again, leaving the body isn't something we tend to remember. Children have brilliant little ways of getting through trauma. I remember being in my body. I remember bare feet on pavement. Warm winter sun through a frosted window. The tricky thing about memory, neuroscientists say, is that often, when we leave our bodies, we lose track of what happens while we are away. This protects us, but leaves us vulnerable. I didn't know how easy it was to leave my body, how effortless, until I couldn't get back in.

Your grandma on your dad's side used to talk about isolation. How life's most painful truth might be that no matter how close we think we are to another person, we are still alone. I didn't want to believe her. I wanted to think I could always see the whole of you. After all, you grew in me.

Then, Arif. Remember, the autumn we binged on *Grey's Anatomy*? Sophie had come home from Smith for a semester because she had all those extra credits, and we needed the savings on tuition, even though she only wanted to stay on campus with her friends. What I knew then: Arif was a college kid—or even older?—who supervised the campaign office where you worked. You were a junior in high school, deep in your policy debate phase, always at practice. Except when you were on the couch with Sophie and me—this was still the old house, soft pink walls glowing and flickering with the TV screen. Meredith and Christina, Meredith and Derek, Meredith and her mother, Meredith and herself, credits rolling, and Sophie—so lovely and amazing in profile—saying, "One more episode?" and me saying, "Just one," and you staring at your phone, fingers tapping out texts. I wanted to leap across the room and pry your phone away and wrap my arms around you like when you were little. Instead, I'd say, "Arif, again?" Then Sophie, "The episode is starting." And you, "I'm fine, Mom." Your hand would rise then to that concave spot at the base of your neck, that hollow V pulsing in and out with every breath.

Milo came after the roses—the ones Mama's first boyfriend gave her at a high school dance. His name was Jon. Which is only funny because my stepdad is also named Jon, and my dad is John. That's a lot of Johns. Anyway, the boyfriend's name was Jon and Mama said he was sweet. And kind. And he gave her roses at the dance. Not just one rose, but a whole bouquet wrapped in pretty paper and crinkly cellophane with a beautiful pattern printed on it. Mama left the roses in the back window of her car, where the sun shone and shone and shone until they were dry and wilted.

Dead.

Actually, Jon wasn't my first boyfriend. He wasn't even my boyfriend—just a nice boy who took me on one date. Not a dance, either—we had dinner at a spaghetti place in a converted fire station that doesn't exist anymore. After that, I hid from him and his niceness. Also, that car was Grandma's, not mine. I didn't have one. But you are right about everything else. And I was wrong to start your story with Arif. After all, your first boyfriend was Graham, from your eighth-grade Waldorf class. Well, first was Sam E. in fourth grade, Sam E. with the shaggy brown hair and that little "oh" of a mouth. He gave you, what was it, a crystal squirrel with blue bead eyes, because you loved all things tiny and fragile. Then Sage, who fell hard for you when he played Tevye opposite your Golde in *Fiddler*. This was before you told me you liked girls, or at least, liked girls more than boys. Before you stopped believing in the line between them. But Graham, he was the first you called a boyfriend, even though I always thought it would be Oscar, with his thick dark hair, charming cowlick, and chipped front tooth. Eventually, it *was* Oscar, when you both ended up at South High after Waldorf. It was bound to happen, the two of you tangled up in each other while I layered lasagna noodles and ricotta cheese into a glass baking pan and wondered if I should or shouldn't keep trudging up and down the stairs to remind you to walk the dog or set the table or whatever other chore I could invent to impose a stopping point before the groping turned to more. Not because I didn't want you to have more, but because I didn't know if that's what *you* wanted. I had yet to ask.

V

Our bodies are a complicated mix of hormones, potent chemical messengers surging through our veins. Our microsystems are continually changing. Impossible to control. There are no hard and fast rules to teach anyone how to recognize what feels good or bad in their bodies. Which is part of why I don't like the "good touch, bad touch" approach to teaching children about boundaries. It's abstract and more rigid than real life. What I know is that human touch is essential to how we grow. Look at Harlow's monkeys. Those cold "mother" bodies made of wire, those frantic infant minds. Touch organizes our emotions, activates our nervous systems, literally paves our neural pathways. Touch calms our souls back into our bodies. At least, it can.

Here's the thing about Arif: he choked you, then claimed you liked it.

We are conditioned to tell children what to do with their bodies.

His hands around your neck, his fingers tightening. Your trachea collapsing in on itself.

Don't put that rock in your mouth. No, you may not jump from that ledge. Let go of her hair, that hurts her body.

You didn't think you liked it, but how could you be sure?

Be polite, we tell them. Wave hello. Stop putting your hand in your pants. Give your uncle a hug.

Arif was so calm. So sure.

Some things we just have to do.

You didn't say a word.

VI.

My story is not my mama's story.

In psychology, the life story model says people in modern societies provide their lives with unity and purpose by constructing internal and evolving narratives of the self. This model explains that identity takes the form of a story, complete with settings, scene, character, plot, and theme.

I remember Mama's stories. And mine. I remember it all.

You don't remember your chicken pox. You were only one year old. But you know the story I've told you so many times, how all three of you kids came down with spots that spring. Yours were the worst. Itchy sores festering everywhere—your scalp, your eyes and nostrils, tummy and thighs, the hollows of your armpits, the crevices between your toes, the folds of your vulva, the soft expanse from clavicle to chin. Even inside your mouth, the whole of it. I soaked you in the bathroom sink—we still lived in the country then, the big house with the black walnut trees—and I had brewed a concoction from plantain leaves, known for cooling and soothing. I kissed the top of your head and tucked strands of baby hair behind your ears. I played pat-a-cake with your fat little hands to keep you from scarring yourself forever.

On my off days, or when I was scared, Mama would rub my back. She still does. Just the right amount of pressure, big circles repeating themselves over and over across my skin. My breath would slow, an ocean inside my chest. I was inside my body. My Self with a capital S—that's what Mama says—would push against the boundaries of my skin. I would curl up on the couch, head pushed into a throw pillow, floral pattern blooming around my face and tangled hair. I never wanted

to go up to my bed. The couch was better. It was my boat, rocked by
the currents of human bodies moving around me, floating in a sea of
muffled sound, but, mostly, Mama's voice.

When I'm scared, I freeze. Your brother and I were at the U of
M on a soaking March day, wending our way through the student union by Starbucks, when Max pointed. "Arif," he said. My
legs dissolved and gravity made an anchor of my body. The atrium
cracked open into silence as the fluorescence grayed around the
periphery. I wondered if we should confront him. "I might lose it,"
Max said. "I'd have to be ready to lose it." College kids flowed past
us like a river, their shoulders curled under heavy backpacks. They
parted around our bodies like water around a boulder, the girls'
fruity shampoo engulfing everything, their glossy hair swaying as if
alive, their nude lips pursed as if they already knew.

VII.

Mama was with Cyrus before my dad. Cyrus drove a hearse and lived in the basement of a funeral home. Mama thought she loved him. She would have had the baby if Cyrus hadn't said no, absolutely not. Cyrus wasn't as kind as Jon, who gave Mama the roses. Which was good, because Mama knew about the hurt inside her, how she didn't deserve perfect beautiful things. Cyrus didn't have an ex-wife or kids, either, which was also good. Mama didn't want to write another sad apology letter to her Spanish teacher/part-time mother who didn't approve of Mama spending time with "that type of man"—a man like Milo. Cyrus was just the right amount of broken.

It was Eve, not my Spanish teacher, who was horrified about Milo. She had moved back from Mexico by then, and I introduced Milo to her, which went poorly. Also, Cyrus didn't live in the basement of that funeral home. His best friend did, though, and I spent many late nights on the other side of the morgue wall, watching them get high and play Dungeons and Dragons. As for your friend Jacob, he lived at that rental house over in Como where all the debate boys played video games—the house where they threw that big party at the beginning of summer. I knew you and Jacob had a thing. But at least Jacob was your age. At least you could be his equal. At least he couldn't deny your intelligence, the ferocity of your mind. That's what I thought. You'd had a lot to drink by the time he took you upstairs, so much that the room liquified and the waves slapped the edges of the bed and made your stomach roll in that part pain part pleasure way and you were a little seasick and the air was dark and humid and sour with booze and it was hard and it was fast and it hurt and it was over. The next morning you rode your bike alone to Walgreens and bought Plan B and stopped talking to Jacob. You only told me weeks later on a scorching July afternoon. I held your flushed cheeks between my palms. "This is your body," I said. "I made you from scratch."

I wish there was a simple pictograph that could lay out where our limits should be. Like the face charts we use in preschool to teach children how to identify their emotions. You can give yourself up, sacrifice yourself for something until your face looks like this smiley, no, this one, right here, then you say stop.

By the time of Ryan, your debate coach, you were eighteen, about to graduate. I remember the June night you told me, the way the sun melted behind the red metal roof of our neighbor's house and bounced all that warm light through our picture window. Your cheeks radiated as if that light shone from inside your body. The TV was on—some news report about yet another high school teacher in a sex scandal with a student. I said *how awful, how awful.* And the lamp inside you switched off as you left the room, pounded up the stairs. I found you face down on your bed, crying. "Mama," you said, "don't you know I love Ryan? And I need you to love him, too? I need you and Sophie to love him and be happy for me, for us. I need that, Mama, I need it."

What does it mean to be autonomous? To have the right to decide what we want and how we want it? When are we not *compromising some desire, some comfort or need, for something or someone else?*

I haven't even mentioned Ethan. Remember when we went to the mall—it was the end of your junior year—to get you some "business casual" clothes for a debate tournament in Georgia? Right before you won the state tournament, got that college scholarship? Anyway, you and Ethan had been together—was it a year already?—and I had taken you to the doctor for birth control. You told me, as we drove home that day, past Pier One and Second Wind Sports, that Ethan didn't like talking about sex. "He gets embarrassed," you said. "But, I told him, look, if we can't talk about it, we shouldn't be doing it." You laughed and I laughed and my heart was so full, because your words sounded like a shield, or a net, or a spell, something stronger than I'd dared to hope. That's what I was thinking as the gray ribbon of highway stretched out behind us and you opened the window of the Prius and threw your bare feet onto the dashboard, a thing I'd warned you so many times not to do, because of that YouTube video, the one showing how dangerous this carefree gesture can be, how in the event of a crash it can buckle your legs, shatter them on impact, explode your bones in all directions, like stars.

VIII.

Mama says I came from the stars. But I know I came from her. I have Mama's mouth and teeth. I have her voice.

You've heard this one before.

The Mafia story.

No. The one where you slid out of me so fast the nurse was caught off guard. Begged me frantically not to push, even though I was already pushing with everything I had.

His booming voice and hairy hands. How he put Auntie on the hood of the car to stop Grandma from driving away after the worst fight, the bloody one. How he plunked Auntie down in her diaper on the hot metal and said, "Going somewhere? Not so fast."

So fast the doctor almost didn't make it, wasn't even in scrubs. So fast he could barely catch you. You've heard how I shook so hard once you came out that the bed rocked and banged against the wall.

How Mafia broke things—heavy wooden cabinets and tables. How he hurt and hurt and hurt. I know all the stories. How all that hurt grew into Mama. How she soaked it up through her spine.

How I could barely keep you in my arms, between your slipperiness and my shaking. How the nurse had to lean over my right shoulder—her clean, soapy smell—to help me hold you. How I nestled you in my arms and the nurse nestled us in her arms, and I kissed your damp head and vowed with all my heart never to let anything hurt you, including me. An impossible vow I knew I would break, because I had already broken it time and again with your sister and brother.

IX.

It was impossibly beautiful, my rose. I clutched it in my warm fists, held myself tall and still in the backseat, so careful not to crush its tender petals. I was given this rose on the first day of first grade during a welcome ceremony.

I cried when you were born.

I walked through a bridge of rainbow silks in my Mary Janes to the sound of my teacher's voice, singing.

I cried for your tiny arms, fragile as wings. Even through the riot of my trembling, your flesh—pillowy soft and still waxy with vernix—was instantly familiar. The feeling of you was exactly as I remembered the feeling of my Nana, the one who loved me best, when I was small.

The rose was perfect and red. At home, Mama helped me put it in a tall clear vase that ruffled at the top. When my rose began to die, as all things do, Mama tied a ribbon around its stem and hung it upside down in the kitchen. "This way, you can keep it forever."

For a long time, I held you like that, fresh born and calm. I searched the open water of your eyes.

Flowers soak up whatever we put in their vases.

"I know you, little baby," I said. "I'm so glad you came."

Rock on Bone

One day when I was three years old, I tripped while running on the sidewalk. Before I fell, I flew, flew in my brown saddle shoes with their slick leather soles and loose laces, my white acrylic knee-highs slouched around my ankles. Sloping above me, the ancient glacial rock of Lake Superior's North Shore, dandelion and lupine sprouting from its crevices. Below me, another heaving, cracked-up sidewalk like all the others then and now in the West End of Duluth, Minnesota. When I ran, I soared. When I crashed, I crashed.

There was loose gravel on the sidewalk, and a round pebble lodged itself under the skin of my split knee. No one washed the cut. The blood dried, my knee scabbed over, the split skin fused itself back together, but the pebble remained, a pea-sized bump. For many years, I could wiggle the hidden pebble from side to side with my finger. The sensation of rock on bone was pleasantly painful, a sharp surprise.

One day the pebble dissolved. I don't know exactly when, because it left a hard lump of scar tissue in its place, which itself softened only slowly, over time, so that the moment of its gone-ness was unknowable, even to me.

Author's Note

While these stories are all true, not everything I have depicted is entirely factual. In some cases, I have condensed and conflated certain events, combined two characters into one, changed names and identifying characteristics to protect privacy, and retold family lore (always identified as such) as I remember hearing it, without having been able to confirm all of the details. I have also attempted to recreate the essence of truthful dialogue even knowing that none of us remember exact words uttered decades ago. Ultimately, I've done my best to chart the course of an early trauma, a cellular memory that runs like a river through my veins, and, therefore, my children's veins. Of course, we know that memory is fluid, nonlinear, mutable. Memories change and reform themselves in response to external influences, including new experiences and relationships. Memories overlap and tangle up with one another. They replicate imperfectly. That is to say, with the passage of any time at all, we remember not actual events, but, rather, memories of events, followed by memories of memories of events, and so on, with each iteration altered by myriad factors, including not only our perspective when remembering, but also the conflicting memories of influential others who have a stake in the same story. In the end, that's what these remembered fragments are really about: the shape-shifting and elliptical nature of memory juxtaposed with particular and unalterable truths that live permanently, and mysteriously, within our bodies.

Acknowledgments

Without my mother's flair for storytelling, and her enduring passion for education, I might never have tilted toward words, might never have crouched down to look at them up close, to look harder, "with my eyes," until they opened up, one by one, and showed me inside their enchanted world. For that, I am profoundly grateful. And Dorothy Allison. I was twenty-four with babies on both hips when *Bastard Out of Carolina* taught me that a person can forge pain into something else entirely—something still painful, but also potentially luminous for another. Dorothy is the reason I first tried to write this book, and the reason I kept trying for all the years it took to find a way. Her enthusiastic support for this work at Tin House in 2016 was fundamental to my completion of it. Likewise, Paul Matthews's strange and marvelous writing workshop in 2009 fundamentally altered my understanding of what writing is and can be, a shift without which I would never have been able to write about my childhood.

As for the editorial team at Split/Lip Press, I have been in awe of them since the moment Kristine Langley Mahler's publication offer arrived just as I first held a newborn granddaughter—such boundless hope and possibility—against my chest. Kristine saw the light in this manuscript, then found crucial ways to clarify and brighten it. She also allowed far more latitude with additions and changes than any writer deserves. Kristine, I bow to you! And to Caleb and David, too, who took extraordinary care to create a beautiful book inside and out. And Allison and Mandana for championing its arrival into the world.

I am grateful to the journals in which some early versions of these chapters appeared, including *North American Review, Calyx, december*, *Up the Staircase Quarterly*, *Nowhere*, *The Doctor T.J. Eckleburg Review*, *Proximity*, and the *Minneapolis Star-Tribune*. Oceans of love for the editors and judges who selected various chapters as contest winners or finalists—particularly Joyce Carol Oates, Jo Ann Beard, and Paul Lisicky.

Without Vermont College of Fine Arts and its magical hilltop campus, this book would not have coalesced. I am deeply thankful to my advisors Martha Southgate, Brian Leung, Richard McCann, and—especially and eternally—the brilliant Sue William Silverman, who believed in me and my work and compelled me to do the same, even when the work was hard indeed.

I am grateful for support from Brush Creek Foundation for the Arts, where I wrote in the shadow of the mountains in a studio surrounded by sage and mule deer. Those mule deer, with a bit of imagination, looked almost like jackalope. Residencies can be lonely, and I was lucky to find wonderful companionship, especially from Sky and Jan, who made endless bowls of instant vegetarian noodles more exciting, wild dogs less scary, and curious-eyed horses more thrilling. Likewise, I am grateful to Millay Colony for the Arts, where I wrestled with this story in a second-floor studio in the barn that Edna St. Vincent Millay built from a Sears Roebuck kit. During that blisteringly hot July, I found immeasurable solace in the friendship and insight of visual artist Kelly Popoff, the only other mother in residence. Kelly, you heard the minor-key in these pages, and the rising chord. How you captured that in your sublime cover art, I will never know, but thank you, thank you, thank you.

This work also benefited from the wise critiques of my many workshop colleagues at VCFA and Tin House; I am indebted to you all. And, Hallie, you generously pushed me to ask for the one thing I most wanted for this book when I thought it couldn't be had. You deserve every good thing—please keep writing. Tom and Kris, where would I be today had you not hired me when I was just a baby writer? My early publishing with you helped open doors toward what my life has become.

Of course, a book doesn't get onto shelves and into readers hands without a whole lot of help, and I am so lucky to have had such expert guidance and support from Jill Swenson, Kristina Marie Darling, Eva Mulloy, and the binders. I'd have collapsed trying to do this alone. To the Elephant Rock writers: the way you looked at me when I read from these pages changed everything. My life is richer for your voices and your presence. Zoe and Liza, you too—here's to many grand adventures to come!

As for my sisters, you will always be my heroes. L, you never stop leading by example, cutting the path, and setting the bar. Who knows what kind of thicket I'd be stuck in had it not been for you, were it not still for you. R, your love of this work and your joy in seeing yourself in it gave me courage I dearly needed. Sorry about all the truancy and prank calling. Nana and Lala, I hope you somehow know, wherever you are, what your love meant. And I hope I brought you a fraction of the astonishing joy my grandchildren now bring me.

To my giant, complicated, wacky, and wonderful OZ family, you are my breath, every single one of you, by blood, marriage, and choice. My rhymes and my reasons are and always will be you: the ones who first made me a mother, and the ones who later made room for me. S, thank you for your brilliant and astute reads, over and over again, for your ALL-CAPS replies, and, most of all, for being brave enough to come first. L, you didn't just find the "little white teeth," which was spectacularly helpful in itself, but you also found a way to lead me back to the world through the work when I was broken. There will never be words for that. M, do you remember when you said you were proud of me? I needed that so much more than you knew. Middle to middle, monkey to monkey, heart to heart forever and ever. And Jon—I do see that horizon now, I see the whole of it, and always will, because of you.

About the Author

Jeannine Ouellette's work has appeared widely in journals including *North American Review, Narrative, Calyx, Masters Review, Writer's Chronicle, december*, and others, as well many anthologies such as *Ms. Aligned: Women Writing About Men, Nowhere Print Annual, Women's Lives: Multicultural Perspectives*, and *Feminist Parenting*. She has received fellowships from Millay Colony and Brush Creek, and her stories and essays have won recognition from the *Narrative* Story Contest, *Masters Review* fiction contest, *Calyx*'s Margarita Donnelly Award for Prose, *december*'s Curt Johnson Prose Award, and more. Jeannine lives in Minneapolis near the banks of the Mississippi, where she teaches writing through the Minnesota Prison Writing Workshop and the University of Minnesota, as well as through Elephant Rock, the independent writing program she founded in 2012.

Now Available From

Split/Lip Press

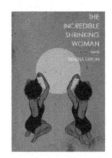

For more info about the press and our titles, visit

www.splitlippress.com

Follow us on Twitter and Instagram: @splitlippress

Made in USA - Kendallville, IN
1222839_9781952897061
01 07 2021 1420